International Accounting
and Financial Reporting

Norlin G. Rueschhoff

The Praeger Special Studies program—utilizing the most modern and efficient book production techniques and a selective worldwide distribution network—makes available to the academic, government, and business communities significant, timely research in U.S. and international economic, social, and political development.

International Accounting and Financial Reporting

PRAEGER SPECIAL STUDIES IN INTERNATIONAL BUSINESS, FINANCE, AND TRADE

Praeger Publishers   New York   London

Library of Congress Cataloging in Publication Data

Rueschhoff, Norlin G
    International accounting and financial reporting.

    (Praeger special studies in international business, finance,
and trade)
    Bibliography: p.
    Includes index.
    1. International business enterprises—Accounting.
2. Accounting. 3. Financial statements. 4. Foreign
exchange—Accounting. I. Title.
HF5657.R83   657   76-12871
ISBN 0-275-23110-0

PRAEGER PUBLISHERS
200 Park Avenue, New York, N.Y. 10017, U.S.A.

Published in the United States of America in 1976
by Praeger Publishers, Inc.

789   038   98765432

Dedicated to
G.T.F., J.C., T.H.S., S.J.T., and M.G.A.

PREFACE

This book is a comprehensive introduction to international accounting. It provides a focus on the many accounting issues that the aspiring international accountant should study. The book may be as much a part of an office collection of an international financial executive as it would be for a library of an international accountant. Further, it may be used in a separate international accounting course, or as supplementary reading in advanced accounting theory courses in the financial or managerial area at undergraduate or graduate levels.

Accountants of the future will be involved constantly in the coordination and stimulation of world economic growth through the use of financial statements as communicative devices. Worldwide reporting objectives will be pursued in such a way that world resources can be shared as effectively and justly as possible. Regulative restrictions imposed by the profession on itself and its clients will continue to be established to present truth and fairness. Understanding future international dimensions can thus be fruitful for the public accountant, the management consultant, the financial executive, the industrial accountant, the internal auditor, the tax expert, or the federal government accountant. That is why the international accounting perspective is being introduced and broadened increasingly at the undergraduate, as well as at the graduate level.

International accounting is not a separate discipline. It covers the entire accounting spectrum. In this study, it broadly includes: accounting for international activities; multinational enterprise accounting control; comparative worldwide accounting principles; and transnational financial reporting for investors. As outlined in introductory Part I, there is a balance between managerial and financial accounting and between external and internal reporting. Part II presents financial accounting problems in international activities, extending beyond the material generally covered in advanced accounting texts. While reviewing the traditional concepts, it includes coverage of accounting for forward exchange contracts, the unique practicalities in the application of the cost-or-market rule to foreign inventories, and an introduction into international tax considerations.

Multinational enterprise control, discussed in Part III, has been given tremendous consideration since the 1960s; these chapters provide some insights into the intricacies of controlling the multinational enterprise and the utility of an adequate internal reporting system.

Part IV discusses comparative international accounting principles, offering the reader a breadth of view seldom given to the accounting scholar in the past. An overview of the generally accepted worldwide accounting principles and emerging social accounting concepts provides many intriguing subjects for broad discussion, and shows that accounting will achieve new horizons in the future.

Part V shows the current efforts to provide more meaningful financial statements for the international investor; eventually the controversies now presented will subside, allowing for international harmonization. But until there are established international audit standards and consistent financial reporting, an understanding of opposing views will be as necessary for the education of the future accountant as it is for the accountant involved in international cooperation today.

Many ideas for this work were fermented in the classroom and with academic colleagues at international accounting seminars and committee meetings. Many of the refinements may be attributed to the information supplied by international financial executives and to my research experiences. I am thankful for the manuscript typing efforts of Esther Cyr. Thanks are also extended for the materials furnished by the international accounting firms.

CONTENTS

LIST OF EXHIBITS

xi

INTRODUCTION

1

THE INTERNATIONAL ACCOUNTING FUNCTION

The need for international accounting expertise is not to have an accountant who specializes in the financial, economic, and legal activities of a particular region. Rather, international accounting knowledge will aid the professional accountant in his international financial responsibilities.

A number of international business trends show the growing magnitude of the need for international accounting expertise. These trends include a continuous expansion of international trade and operations by U.S. firms. Firms both within and outside the United States are becoming larger and more multinational in scope, and the world's industrial giants outside the United States are gaining strength. There is also a rise in the interchange of foreign stockholdings—that is, there are more and more foreigners buying U.S. stocks as well as U.S. citizens investing abroad. These trends suggest the added responsibilities of, and prospective directions for, the international accountant.

THE INTERNATIONAL ACCOUNTING STRUCTURE

At the microlevel, international accounting comprises accounting for firm-level business activity that crosses national boundaries or is conducted in a location other than the firm's domicile country. This excludes the elements of foreign legal, political, economic, and social environments except as these elements affect the accounting function of the international business firm. It also excludes the knowledge of accounting principles of a given country unless it relates to international business activity. The study of comparative accounting principles is, however, an element of international accounting since it is related to transnational financial reporting for investors.

EXHIBIT 1.1

Multinational Enterprise Accounting Tasks

Corporate Level Assignments

Controllership	Treasurership
1. Consolidations policy and procedures (for example, translation methods, which affiliates to include in consolidation).	1. Provision of capital for projects and unusual cash needs (for example, bank loans for medium- and long-term financing, bond issued, stock issued).
2. Formulation and installation of standard chart of accounts.	2. Coordination of short-term financing to insure optimum use of working capital on a global basis (for example, maximum use of overdraft where necessary, and standards for dividend payment).
3. Accounting procedures and techniques (for example, depreciation methods for types of assets, inventory valuation).	
4. Internal auditing techniques and procedures.	3. Policies and procedures for protection of exposed assets, inflationary countries, and currency deterioration.
5. Format and timing of operating and capital budgets.	4. Relations with domestic and foreign bankers.
6. Format and timing of reporting and control systems.	5. Stockholder relationships throughout the world.
7. Selection and use of EDP equipment for the accounting function (for example, use of standard hardware and programing).	6. Policy and procedures for credit and collections (to insure that multidivision customers do not exceed normal credit lines, and to standardize risk limits).
8. Selection of local certified public accountants for foreign subsidiaries.	7. Policy and procedure on investments to be made with excess cash (for example, what types of securities are acceptable, what balance should be in the portfolio).
	8. Insurance coverage (a function often assumed by corporate staff to take advantage of overall or blanket policies that can reduce insurance costs).

Divisional Assignments

1. Guidelines for formulation of subsidiary budgets.
2. Review and consolidation of subsidiary budgets.
3. Analysis of subsidiary performance, and action recommendations.
4. Advisory services and training for subsidiary controlling.
5. Establishment of divisional controllership policies.
6. Supervision of pricing practices.

1. Review of cash and working capital positions and recommendations.
2. Review of exposed asset protection.
3. Coordination of borrowing practices.
4. Advisory and training services for subsidiary treasurers.

Subsidiary Assignments

1. Preparation of financial reports and consolidation.
2. Analysis of financial performance.
3. Preparation of budgets and financial forms.
4. Maintenance of books, ledgers, journals, accounting records, including EDP equipment.
5. Auditing of subsidiary operations.
6. Preparation of tax returns.

1. Analysis of working capital needs and cash requirement forecasts.
2. Day-to-day banking operations for short-term funds.
3. Operations to protect exposed assets.
4. Administration of credit and collection operations.
5. Investment of excess cash in approved investments.
6. Provision of local insurance policies and contracts.

Source: Business International, *Organizing for International Finance*, Management Monograph no. 35 (New York: Business International, 1966), pp. 21-23.

5

Certainly, then, international accounting is not a separate discipline. It encompasses all areas of accounting—managerial accounting, financial accounting, accounting theory, auditing, and taxes. In this book, international accounting includes four categories: accounting for international operations; multinational accounting control; international financial reporting; and comparative international accounting principles. The first two are primarily internal accounting—financial and managerial—and the latter two, external reporting theory and practice. Auditing principles and standards are part of international financial reporting. Tax problems are integrated throughout.

DUTIES OF THE INTERNATIONAL ACCOUNTANT

The duties of the accountant within the international firm are both managerial and financial. On the financial side, the accountant is responsible for the accountability or stewardship of the firm's assets; on the managerial side, for supplying accounting information to assist in management decision making.

The stewardship task in an international firm requires a knowledge of the principles and practices of accounting for international activities. The decision-making task involves multinational accounting control, sometimes referred to as international financial management. These duties are divided between the controller and the treasurer. They are carried out not only at the top level but throughout the lower levels of the multinational organization. The delegation of these tasks among the various levels can be viewed in Exhibit 1.1, which represents the experiences of a broad cross section of international companies.

The stewardship function enables both internal and external parties to evaluate a firm's financial performance and position. The audit of this function is performed by outside auditors. In contrast, outside management consultants may be engaged to assist in monitoring and establishing information systems for routine control decisions as well as to solve major investment and financing problems. The interrelationship of these functions is diagramed in Exhibit 1.2. However, these functions are not confined to internal management objectives but are extended to reporting to investors and other interested parties.

The investors in an international firm may be stockholders, creditors, or others who have indirect claims on the enterprise. Other interested parties include governmental agencies, employees and their labor unions, customers, and suppliers. The creditors and stockholders may be private individuals, institutional investors, or, as may be more prevalent in international operations than in domestic operations, a governmental partner. External reporting to a worldwide audience of such breadth creates problems and requires an understanding that is much broader and deeper than the mere knowledge of the accounting principles and practices within one's own country.

EXHIBIT 1.2

Role of the International Accountant

	Financial Accounting	Management Accounting
Internal Reporting	Treasurer	Controller
External Reporting	Certified Auditor	Management Consultant

Source: Compiled by the author.

International uniformity of accounting principles may seem to be a desirable step toward worldwide reporting to investors. But before there can be uniformity there must be an understanding of the principles of the various countries. These principles must be studied in a comparative manner rather than individually so that one can view the reasons and need for diversity in certain areas or departures from generally accepted principles in certain countries. Indeed, there is now a lack of uniformity in most countries, and many do not consider complete uniformity a desirable objective.

A presently attainable goal is that of full disclosure in reporting, The Eurobond market exemplifies a successful nongovernment-controlled market which would not have been possible without full disclosure in financial reporting to international investors. But even with full disclosure, there are the problems of translation and consolidation.

THE REQUIRED INTERNATIONAL ACCOUNTING EXPERTISE

The international accountant's knowledge must extend into all areas of accounting, for all types of firm-level business activity that crosses national boundaries or is conducted in a location other than the firm's domicile country. This requires cognizance of international financial reporting for investors as well as accounting for management.

The international accountant must provide financial reports that are readily understood by investors around the world. Since international business activity is growing, he must know the financial reporting standards for international business transactions and investments. The increased interchange of foreign stockholdings among the citizens of the world requires that accounting principles be applied in a clear manner so that the financial statement reader may be provided with digestible data.

The role of the multinational enterprise's accountant is to provide the accounting information for the stewardship, operational control, and investment problem-solving tasks of the international firm. The continued rate of expansion of international investments and trade in many firms requires the understanding of problems unique to accounting for international operations.

A knowledge of the current international accounting issues will strengthen international understanding. The improvement of international financial reporting will help the movement of economic trade and investment. Interrelationships in economic and financial affairs as well as in political and social affairs among citizens of various countries may even aid in achieving an international peace.

ACCOUNTING FOR
INTERNATIONAL ACTIVITIES

CHAPTER

2

FOREIGN EXCHANGE

A tourist acquires foreign coins and currency notes in the foreign exchange market. An importer or exporter needing foreign currency to acquire imported goods or to convert foreign currency acquired in the sale of exports must deal with the foreign exchange market mechanism. The foreign exchange market is indeed the most basic element involved in international business transactions.

The foreign exchange market determines the rate at which one currency is exchanged for another currency. Foreign exchange rates as determined by this market are used for the determination of exchange prices in the recording of international business transactions. Foreign exchange rates also are used to measure the amounts of foreign currency items, such as unsettled open account balances, which are reported in financial statements. Within the foreign currency market is the forward market which permits hedging against the exchange rate risks in the holding of open account balances.

FOREIGN EXCHANGE TERMINOLOGY

Foreign exchange consists of the moneys of another country offered for sale in the money market of a given country. Thus in the United States, the purchase or sale of British pound sterling or Mexican pesos for U.S. dollars constitutes foreign exchange. In a similar way, the purchase or sale of U.S. dollars in the London market would constitute foreign exchange to the British businessman.

Not all international business transactions require the use of foreign exchange. A U.S. exporter may sell goods to a French importer and receive payment in French francs. If the U.S. exporter then uses the French francs to purchase French goods which he imports, no foreign exchange is utilized. The French franc, in this case, is France's local currency.

The term local currency, as used in this book, is defined as currency of a specific foreign country. Local currency is distinguished from foreign currency, which is any currency other than the local currency. For example, the local currency for West Germany is the German mark; for Great Britain, it is the pound sterling. However, from the standpoint of the United States, both German marks and pound sterling are foreign currencies. Also, in West Germany, the pound sterling is a foreign currency.

Accountants are concerned with the recording of foreign exchange transactions and of transactions involving foreign and local currencies. When one currency is actually exchanged for another, the exchange is a conversion. Thus, conversion is the term used to describe money changing.

Accountants must also record transactions in foreign currencies where no money changing, no conversion, takes place. In the above instance of a U.S. exporter acquiring French francs for his goods, the transaction is recorded in U.S. dollars—the currency of his domicile enterprise; it becomes necessary to translate the French franc payment into U.S. dollars in order to record the settlement on the exporter's records. Thus, a foreign currency transaction is translated into the currency commonly used by the businessman. Financial statements are also translated.

INSTRUMENTS OF FOREIGN EXCHANGE

Bank Transfers

The main device for effecting foreign exchange transactions is the bank transfer. The principal method of transferring a deposit to or from a bank abroad is a cable transfer over the ocean or telegraphic transfer over land. Such transfer can also be made by mail. However, the speed of a cable or telegraphic transfer gives them tremendous advantage over the mail transfer.

A cable transfer is an order transmitted by cable to a foreign correspondent bank to make payment to a designated payee. It directs the foreign bank to debit the account of the seller of a particular currency and to credit the account designated by the buyer. Thus, the U.S. exporter who receives a Paris bank deposit in French francs in payment for his goods may desire to sell the francs by means of a cable transfer to his New York bank account in dollars. The conversion rate for the transfer is determined by the current market rate between the two currencies. If the exporter has no French franc bank account, he may ask the payer to transfer the amount by cable directly to his New York bank, which purchases the exchange and credits the equivalent dollars to the exporter's account. The cost of sending the cable is charged by the bank to the sender.

Bills of Exchange

In addition to the cable, telegraphic, or mail transfers of bank balances, there are various bills of exchange used as foreign exchange instruments. Among these, checks, money orders, and sight drafts effect immediate cash payments; time drafts provide for deferred payments.

Personal checks have become increasingly important as a means of international cash payment, and those of reputable international corporations are commonly accepted in all parts of the world. Dividend and bond interest payments are often sent by check to foreign stockholders and bondholders as well as to domestic holders. Travelers checks and money orders in hard currencies are also widely accepted.

The acceptor of the check normally sells it to his local bank for local currency. The local bank, in turn, sends the check to its foreign correspondent bank in the country of the check's currency. There it is presented to the drawee bank for payment and credit to the correspondent bank's account.

Bank drafts, similar to checks, are used when a foreigner wants to remit funds directly without going through a foreign bank. A New York bank may sell a French purchaser of U.S. goods a draft on the bank's balance abroad. Many U.S. banks have overseas branches for such purposes. The draft may then be mailed directly to the U.S. exporter who is able to cash it like any other check.

Other bills of exchange regularly used in international commerce are sight drafts and time drafts. A sight draft is an order drawn by a domestic bank upon a foreign correspondent bank to pay on demand a certain sum in money to the bearer or to the order of a designated payee. The use of drafts has evolved mostly in the commercially developed countries. One type of draft, the commercial bill, arises when an exporter draws a draft directly on the foreign purchaser for the amount of the export sale.

Through the issuances of letters of credit, a banker's bill becomes another type of draft. A banker's bill arises when the exporter draws a draft directly on the foreign purchaser's bank or its correspondent bank. The letter of credit (examined in Chapter 3) is an assurance by the bank that a designated party's check or draft will be paid by the bank upon presentation. If a letter of credit is issued, the exporter has greater assurance of collection for the goods shipped to the foreign purchaser.

Usually, a banker's bill or commercial bills are documentary bills. That is, a bill of lading or other document of title for the goods accompanies the draft. The title document is to be surrendered only after the draft is paid if it is a sight draft, or accepted if it is a time draft.

Time drafts are similar to sight drafts except that, instead of being payable on demand, they are payable a certain number of days after presentation. Commercial letters of credit previously given to the exporter assure him that the time draft will be paid at the end of a 30-, 60-, 90-, or 180-day period. Time drafts, like sight drafts, can be documentary bills, but they may also be "clean" bills. Clean bills unaccompanied by title documents are utilized if the exporter is willing to pass title to the goods prior to payment or acceptance by the foreign purchaser or his bank.

Foreign Currency Notes and Coins

Besides the use of bank transfers and bills of exchange, foreign transactions can also be settled by payment in the actual currency, that is, the currency notes and coins, of the foreign country. Tourists traveling abroad use this means of international cash payment as their chief foreign exchange instrument. Also U.S. merchants and others, particularly in the border areas, use a fairly large volume of Canadian currency. The use of foreign currency notes as an instrument of foreign exchange is an important one, but it is practically limited to smaller transactions.

FOREIGN EXCHANGE RATES

Market rates

The market rates for foreign exchange vary slightly for the different foreign exchange instruments. The *Wall Street Journal*, for example, regularly quotes the selling prices for bank transfers in the United States for payment abroad, the buying and selling prices for foreign bank notes in New York, and the bid and asked prices for U.S. dollars and Canadian dollars in London. These are spot prices quoted for immediate delivery in the interbank market. The rates for cable transfers are the basic spot rates; the rates for other transactions, such as mail transfers or bills of exchange, are based on the cable transfer rate. Since the cable transfer is the main device for currency conversion, the spot rate becomes the most relevant to financial accounting measurement.

In the interbank or wholesale market, the banks ordinarily do not charge a commission on the foreign exchange transactions. The small spread between the buying and selling rates provides the revenue for the bank. This spread includes the foreign exchange broker's commission which must be paid on transactions between the banks.

The bank's rates for customers tend to be less favorable than the cable transfer rates. Nevertheless, competition is keen among the bankers in the retail market. The bulk of the foreign exchange business with firms and individuals is transacted by telephone. Many firms shop around for the best price before making the actual sale or purchase. Though the quoting of the rate is nearly automatic, it represents a careful assessment of the market factors as weighted with the customer's present and potential business. The foreign exchange trader knows the current state of the market, its expected future trend, and the current exchange position of the bank.

Differential Rates

A few currencies are traded in a black market, but the most prominent divergent exchange rates are local government sponsored. Governments often establish special rates for specified transactions. The rates may be classified as preferential or penalty rates; both are quite prevalent in Latin America.

Preferential rates are in effect favorable rates. They are established for essential or desirable imports which are differentiated from less preferred imports and dividend remittances. These preferential rates act as a form of government subsidy to maintain lower selling prices to the public in a foreign country. Rebates are sometimes also given to encourage imports of essential foods.

Penalty rates are less favorable than the free market and official exchange rates. They constitute a tax on imports. In some cases, the difference is actually levied as a tax. Also, the purchase of the proceeds from exports of designated products by the central banks at specified less favorable rates constitutes a type of export duty.

Forward Rates

The forward rate is the market rate for forward exchange contracts. A forward exchange contract between a bank and a customer or between two banks specifies delivery of a certain sum in foreign currency at a future date and at a designated rate; the rate, designated at the time the contract is made, is the forward rate. The *Wall Street Journal* regularly quotes the forward rate for 30-day and 90-day futures of British pound sterling. Canadian dollars and several continental European currencies are also active in the forward market.

The forward rate designated in the contract may be more or less than the spot rate on the date the contract is made. Similarly, the forward rate may also be more or less than the spot rate on the date the contract must be fulfilled. Most forward exchange contracts are made over the telephone and later confirmed in writing.

If a buyer or seller knows only approximately when the foreign currency is needed or received, he may execute a forward option contract. Such contracts may be arranged for delivery at the beginning of a month (from the first to the tenth), the middle (from the eleventh to the twentieth), or the end (from the twenty-first on), or in another requested period of time. Though in this case the cost to the customer may be slightly higher, the customer does have more leeway in timing.

Forward exchange contracts shift the risk of future purchases or sales of foreign currencies to the banker-dealer. Because of the risk involved, the creditworthiness of the customer is an important element in the forward exchange business. For the customer anticipating the receipt or delivery of foreign exchange, the forward exchange market serves a highly useful purpose.

ACCOUNTING FOR FOREIGN EXCHANGE

The holding of foreign exchange on the balance sheet date must be reflected in the accounts. Foreign exchange is a type of cash account. For external reporting the balance sheet nomenclature "cash on hand and in bank" includes the holdings of any foreign exchange whether in the form of foreign exchange instruments or foreign bank accounts. Blocked currency accounts restricted from conversion into other currencies by the foreign central monetary authority must be disclosed on the balance sheet if the amounts are material. The disclosure may be by footnote, by parenthetical remark, or by setting forth the amount in a separate category.

Recording Foreign Exchange

There are two methods of keeping foreign exchange accounts: the cost method and the standard rate method. The cost method records transactions in both currencies at the actual amounts. The foreign currency columns constitute a perpetual inventory. This method requires an adjustment at the month-end to bring the ending balance in line with the current value of the foreign currency balance. The adjustment is recorded in a foreign exchange gain and loss account.

The standard rate method reduces all transactions to a standard rate. The difference between the standard rate and the actual cost or proceeds is immediately recorded in the exchange gain and loss account. An adjustment is required at month's end only if the standard rate is changed. The standard rate usually represents an average rate around which most current transaction prices are fluctuating. Illustrations of the two methods are presented in Exhibit 2.1.

Recording Forward Exchange Contracts

A forward exchange transaction involves the purchase or sale of foreign exchange for delivery in the future. No cash transaction occurs at the time the contract is negotiated. Definite liabilities exist on the part of both parties. Each party agrees to deliver one foreign currency in exchange for the other currency at the specified rate on the contract's designated date. Each acquires a liability in one currency and a receivable in the other currency.

The entries required for recording a forward exchange contract for the sale of foreign currency for delivery 30 days later at the rate of $2.3995 for LC (local currency) 1.00 are as presented in Exhibit 2.2. If the foreign exchange is not received as expected, the amount would have to be purchased in the foreign exchange market.

In practice, the liability for exchange sold is offset against the amount due from the exchange broker. In other words, the liability for exchange sold is considered to be a contraasset. However, when the liability upon revaluation due to an exchange rate change exceeds the offsetting amount due from the broker, only the net amount shows as a liability and the amount due from the broker becomes a contraliability account. Whether or not the amounts should be fully disclosed would then depend on the materiality of the possible effects on the firm's financial position. Thus, many industrial companies do not record the forward exchange contract at all. These firms would accrue only the net difference between the receivable and the liability at the time of an exchange rate change. Then later only the receipt of the foreign exchange and its conversion into domestic cash would be recorded.

Recording Swap Transactions

Swaps are temporary financial operations most commonly arranged between a parent company and its foreign subsidiary. Under such an arrangement, U.S. dollars would be delivered to the central bank, or in some cases to a private bank, in the foreign country where the subsidiary is located. Then local currency is received by the foreign subsidiary from the bank at a special rate of exchange with the understanding that, at the end of a specified time period, the reverse operation will take place—that is, the bank will return the amount of dollars it received in exchange for the amount of local currency it had delivered.

The recording of a swap arrangement is illustrated in Exhibit 2.3. In order to view the effect of a devaluation, entries show such an effect one year later. This illustrates that a swap agreement can protect the foreign assets in the case of devaluation. Whether the foreign assets are in cash or in another financial asset form makes no difference.

The swap receivable is a dollar receivable whereas the swap payable is due in local currency. It would seem that these amounts are separate assets and liabilities on the balance sheet. However, in consolidated financial statements, corporations generally offset one against the other. In this manner, the swap payable is a type of contingent liability, similar in nature to discounted notes receivable. If the amounts are material, full disclosure would be necessary.

EXHIBIT 2.1

Recording Foreign Exchange Ledger Accounts

Cost Method

Date	Explanation	Rate	Foreign Currency			U.S. Dollars		
			Debit	Credit	Balance	Debit	Credit	Balance
December 1	Cable transfer	5.00	3,500		3,500	17,500		17,500
December 10	Sight draft	4.99		400	3,100		1,996	15,504
December 23	30-day draft	4.95	500		3,600	2,475		17,979
December 31	Adjustment	4.99			3,600		15	17,964

Standard Rate Method

Date	Explanation	Rate	Actual Value		Standard Rate (4.99)		
			In Foreign Currency	In U.S. Dollars	Debit	Credit	Balance
December 1	Cable transfer	5.00	3,500	17,500	17,465		17,465
December 10	Sight draft	4.99	400	1,996		1,996	15,469
December 23	30-day draft	4.97	500	2,475	2,495		17,964

General Journals

		Cost Method		Standard Rate	
December 1	Foreign exchange	17,500		17,465	
	Exchange gains and losses			35	
	Cash		17,500		17,500
	To record acquisition of foreign exchange with domestic currency.				
December 10	Purchases	1,996		1,996	
	Foreign exchange		1,996		1,996
	To record use of foreign exchange to purchase imported merchandise.				
December 23	Foreign Exchange	2,475		2,495	
	Exchange gains and losses				20
	Accounts receivable		2,475		2,475
	To record acquisition of foreign exchange through settlement of customer's account.				
December 31	Exchange gains and losses	15		15	
	Foreign exchange		15		15
	To adjust foreign exchange balance to current value.				

Source: Compiled by the author.

EXHIBIT 2.2

Recording Forward Contracts

July 1	Accounts receivable	240,000	
	Sales		240,000
	To record sale of exported merchandise payable in sterling; current spot rate is $2.40.		
July 1	Due from exchange broker	239,950	
	Liability for exchange sold		239,950
	To record the sale of LC 100,000, @ $2.3995, delivery to be made on July 31.		
July 31	Foreign exchange	239,900	
	Exchange gains and losses	100	
	Accounts receivable		240,000
	To record the receipt of July 1 invoice payment of LC 100,000 from a customer; the current spot rate, $2.3990.		
July 31	Liability for exchange sold	239,950	
	Foreign exchange		239,900
	Exchange gains and losses		50
	To record delivery of the LC 100,000 to the bank to cover the short sale.		
July 31	Cash	239,930	
	Exchange gains and losses	20	
	Due from exchange broker		239,950
	To record the receipt of cash from the bank for exchange sold on July 1 and delivered this date, less incidental expenses and commission deducted by the bank.		

Alternative to first July 31 entry if invoice payment is not received from the customer on that date:

July 31	Foreign exchange	239,900	
	Cash		239,900
	To record purchase of LC 100,000, @ current spot rate of $2.3990.		

Note: Local currency is indicated by LC.
Source: Compiled by the author.

EXHIBIT 2.3

Recording Swap Arrangements

At time of negotiation:

Swap receivable	10,000	
Cash		10,000

To record the delivery of dollars to foreign central
    bank in a swap agreement to receive the dollars
    upon the return of the local currency within two
    years.

Foreign exchange	10,000	
Swap payable		10,000

To record the receipt of LC 40,000 at an exchange
    rate of LC 4: $1 under the swap agreement that
    $10,000 will be returned upon the delivery of
    LC 40,000 within two years.

Upon revaluation at later balance sheet date:

Foreign exchange gains and losses	2,000	
Foreign exchange		2,000

To record loss on foreign exchange due to devaluation.

Swap payable	2,000	
Exchange gains and losses		2,000

To revaluate the swap payable to current exchange rate
    and record the gain due to the devaluation.

Upon maturity:

Swap payable	8,000	
Foreign exchange		8,000

To record delivery of LC 40,000 in fulfillment of the
    swap agreement.

Cash	10,000	
Swap receivable		10,000

To record receipt of cash in dollars from delivery of
    local currency at exchange rate agreed to in the swap
    agreement.

Source: Compiled by the author.

Reporting Exchange Gains and Losses

As long as there are no restrictions blocking the purchase or sale of the foreign exchange, the foreign exchange instruments are as liquid as other cash items. Any gains or losses from the foreign exchange fluctuations are realized gains and losses. They should be charged against or credited to ordinary operations. If the amounts from the rate fluctuations are material, financial statement disclosure is recommended.

SUMMARY

The main environmental characteristic that is unique to international operations accounting is the foreign exchange market. This market stipulates the foreign exchange rates which are used in the determination of exchange prices and in the measurement in terms of money for financial accounting. The rates are negotiated through the actual conversion of foreign currencies—money changing. But these rates are also used for translation of foreign transactions into a firm's home currency for the businessman's interpretative purposes.

The instruments which provide the mechanism for the foreign exchange market price negotiation are bank transfers, bills of exchange, and foreign currency notes and coins. The main device is the bank cable transfer; personal checks and other bills of exchange are increasing in importance; foreign currency notes and coins are practically limited to small transactions.

The foreign exchange rates vary slightly for the different exchange instruments. Since the cable transfer is the main device in foreign exchange transactions, its price, called the spot price, is the most important for financial accounting recognition. In contrast, the official rate which is set by foreign central monetary authorities has little importance to accounting measurement. In some cases, differential rates, whether preferential or penalty rates, and forward exchange contract rates may be applicable in the recognition of special transactions.

The holding of foreign exchange instruments or bank accounts is reflected in the balance sheet as cash. Though the amounts may be recorded during the accounting period by the cost method or the standard rate method, the balance sheet amount is reflected at the appropriate market rate. Further disclosure is necessary for material amounts of blocked currencies and for forward exchange contracts or swap arrangements which may materially affect the firm's financial position.

3

FOREIGN TRADE AND INVESTMENT

The export and import business of the United States with other parts of the world originated in U.S. colonial days. The procedures for handling foreign trade shipments are rooted in early commercial practices. Modern banking, transportation, and communications has facilitated the negotiation, movement, and financing of foreign trade. The export-import balance of trade is a significant element in the international blance-of-payments position of any country. The importance of foreign trade cannot be overemphasized.

EXPORT-IMPORT FINANCING

Like domestic trade, overseas trade can be financed through open account, consignments of merchandise, or advance cash deposits. However, the greatest part of overseas trade transactions are handled through the use of letters of credit and bank drafts. Each of these financing methods, along with the specialized authority-to-purchase procedure, serves a purpose in foreign trade.

Letters of Credit

A letter of credit is an instrument issued by a bank at the request of one party authorizing that party or a designated second party to draw a check or draft against the bank or one of its correspondents for a designated sum payable on demand, at a specified time, or upon presentation of specified documents which usually give title to the goods. These include the papers covering the shipment, such as the bill of lading, plus other documents essential to the export or import of the goods.

Generally there are three main types of letters of credit: the cash letter of credit, the traveler's letter of credit, and the commercial letter of credit. Each is issued upon the request of an individual after the bank's approval of the individual's application. The cash letter of credit is a definite demand instrument. It expedites international cash payment. The traveler's letter of credit is a variant of the cash letter. It allows a traveler abroad to carry substantial amounts of funds with safety. In effect, it is a worldwide bank account. The person to whom it is issued may draw demand drafts on the issuing bank at any of its foreign branches or correspondents. The cash letter and the traveler's letter may both be classified as commercial letters of credit. However, commercial letters also are executed for delayed international payments. They may be used for exports and for imports.

Commercial Export Letter of Credit

A commercial letter is issued by a bank at the request of a buyer of merchandise in favor of the seller of the merchandise. It provides for payment to the seller upon his presentation of the specified shipping documents. The usual documents are the invoice, the bills of lading, and the insurance policy or certificate. Other required documents may be certificates of origin, weight lists, various types of certificates of analysis, and packing lists.

Export letters of credit may be either revocable or irrevocable letters. The irrevocable letter is either confirmed or unconfirmed. The confirmed irrevocable straight credit is issued by a foreign bank and confirmed irrevocably by the exporter's domestic bank. The domestic bank is obligated to honor drafts against the irrevocable letter of credit. No changes in the terms may be made without the consent of all parties.

The unconfirmed letter of credit may be the domestic bank's own irrevocable commercial letter of credit. Such a letter is similar to the confirmed irrevocable credit except that the latter is the obligation of two banks whereas the bank's own irrevocable letter of credit carries the obligation of only one bank.

The other type of unconfirmed irrevocable letter of credit is the correspondent's irrevocable straight credit. This letter is issued by the foreign bank without the responsibility or engagement of the exporter's domestic bank. The domestic bank simply transmits the advice of its issuance on behalf of the foreign bank. For the exporter, this method is not as preferred as the confirmed irrevocable straight credit or the domestic bank's own irrevocable letter of credit.

The least frequently used method is the revocable letter of credit. Such a letter is unconfirmed, for no bank will guarantee a letter that may be cancelled by the issuing bank. This type of letter usually serves as a means of arranging payment. It provides no protection prior to payment and may be amended or cancelled without the consent of or notice to the beneficiary.

Commercial Import Letter of Credit

The irrevocable import letter of credit is used to finance a large part of the imports into the United States. The irrevocable letter's principal advantage is that it gives the foreign shipper the protection of a bank obligation. Also, the domestic importer is able to use the purchased merchandise as security in obtaining credit to finance the transaction.

The letter of credit may be fixed, revolving, or increased. A fixed letter of credit is for a certain amount and is exhausted when the amount has been drawn or accepted. In a revolving letter of credit, the original amount is replenished after each draft until the expiration date. For an increased letter of credit, each increase is authorized specifically by an amendment. In most cases, the privilege is a matter of continuous agreement between the bank and its customer. The revolving or the increased letter of credit enables the use of the same letter of credit for all transactions with a specified shipper.

Authority to Purchase

Somewhat similar to the commercial letter of credit is the authority to purchase. It is used mainly by Far Eastern banks to finance exports from the United States and other countries. It gives the exporter a specific domestic bank where he may negotiate drafts on the foreign buyer or his bank abroad. It is an authority extended by the foreign bank to a domestic bank to buy the drafts and documents of a specified shipment. The authority to purchase may be issued irrevocably or revocably on the part of the foreign bank. The irrevocable authority to purchase may be confirmed by the domestic bank.

Drafts

A substantial volume of U.S. exports is financed by dollar drafts. For imports, drafts are used only in specific appropriate circumstances. The dollar draft, a foreign exchange instrument, may be either a time draft or a sight draft. In foreign trade transactions, such drafts are often accompanied by the shipping documents.

Advance Deposits

A very small amount of foreign trade is financed by advance deposits. This method is used when credit risks are doubtful. Certain conditions, such as foreign exchange restrictions or political and economic disturbances, may force the seller into negotiating the no-risk transaction by demanding cash in advance.

Credit on Open Account

For a few well-known, reputable international firms, foreign trade is handled on an open account basis, just as domestic transactions are; besides the delayed payment risk associated with domestic transactions, there is the disadvantage in foreign trade of the added time involved in the goods shipment. Without a tangible obligation upon shipment of the goods, the exporter may be hindered in using the immediate export sale as a basis for obtaining credit from a financial institution.

Goods on Consignment

Goods on a consignment basis are usually limited to shipments to foreign branches or subsidiaries. With the credit risks thoroughly examined and known, consignments are occasionally made to select agents, representatives, or import houses abroad. Since a consignment involves no tangible obligation upon shipment, the consignment basis has the same financing disadvantage as the open account credit transaction.

FOREIGN SHIPMENT TERMS

In the negotiating of foreign trade transactions, the quoted price specifically excludes or includes certain related shipping costs. Besides the customary domestic freight shipment terms, FOB (free on board) shipping point and FOB-destination, there are several other terms commonly used in foreign trade practice. They include FAS (free alongside), C&F (cost and freight), and CIF (cost, insurance, and freight). The standard U.S. definitions of the main foreign trade terms used are published by the International Chamber of Commerce.

Just as in domestic trade, the seller must bear all risks and, unless otherwise specified, all costs until title passes to the buyer at the stipulated point of transfer. Export costs include such items as packing, transportation to point of transfer, documentation fees, sailing registration fees, and insurance as designated by the terms. Usually the foreign duties and export taxes must be paid by the buyer.

ACCOUNTING FOR FOREIGN TRADE

Foreign Sales

An exporter may bill the foreign purchaser in domestic currency or foreign currency. If the invoice is in domestic currency—U.S. dollars for a U.S.

exporter—the exporter bears no risk resulting from an exchange rate fluctuation occurring between the date of invoice and the date of payment. The foreign purchaser must pay the amount in U.S. dollars. When export sales are billed in foreign currency, the exchange gain or loss deriving from the transaction is a revenue or expense to the exporter.

The following example illustrates the difference that may occur in the two billing methods in a transaction involving a U.S. exporter and a foreign merchant:

		Export Billing in U.S. Currency		Export Billing in Foreign Currency	
July 1	Accounts receivable	11,150		11,150	
	Sales		11,150		11,150
	To record the sale of merchandise to a foreign company for U.S. $11,150 or LC 10,000, terms net/30 days.				
July 31	Cash (or foreign exchange)	11,150		11,170	
	Exchange gain or loss				20
	Accounts receivable		11,150		11,150
	To record receipt of U.S. $11,150 or LC 10,000 in payment of July 1 invoice; spot exchange rate is U.S. $1.117 = LC 1.00.				

If the exchange rate had declined from the July 1 market rate, an exchange loss would have occurred in the foreign currency billing. No loss or gain appears in the domestic currency billing because the foreign merchants must remit the U.S. dollar amount. At the U.S. $1.117 rate, it actually cost the foreign importer only LC 9,982.10 to remit the U.S. $11,150.

Foreign Purchases

A foreign firm also may invoice a domestic importer in the foreigner's local currency or the importer's local currency. If the foreigner desires to bear no risk in his own country's currency, he will bill in that currency. The importer then must bear the gain or loss from any currency fluctuation between the invoice date and the payment date. If the foreigner bills in the importer's local currency, the foreign seller will take the gain or loss in exchange rate fluctuations between the two currencies.

To show the differences that may occur in the two billing possibilities, the following example illustrates a transaction involving a U.S. importer of goods from a foreign merchant:

		Import Invoiced in U.S. Currency		Import Invoiced in Foreign Currency	
July 1	Purchases	11,150		11,150	
	Accounts payable		11,150		11,150
	To record the purchase of merchandise from a foreign company for LC 10,000 or U.S. $11,150, terms net/ 30 days.				
July 31	Accounts payable	11,150		11,150	
	Exchange gain or loss			20	
	Cash		11,150		11,170
	To record the payment of the July 1 invoice; spot exchange rate is U.S. $1.117 = LC 1.00.				

Since the exchange rate had risen, the billing in foreign currency cost the U.S. importer an exchange loss. By purchasing the foreign currency forward, he could have avoided the loss. A loan in the foreign currency is another means to hedge against such losses. In this case, the billing in U.S. dollars netted the foreign merchant only LC 9,982.10; he had to absorb the exchange loss because of the decline in the value of the U.S. dollar in relation to the foreign currency.

Exchange Gains and Losses

In the illustrations above, the exchange gains or losses were recorded as revenue or expense of the current period. Several theoretical questions may arise concerning the acceptance of this principle. They include the proper income or expense classification, and the allocation of the income or expense if the fluctuation occurs among two or more accounting periods. In connection with the allocation question, there is the problem as to when the gain or loss becomes realized and whether any unrealized gain or loss should be recorded. These are financial reporting problems.

An alternative to reporting the exchange gain or loss separately could be charging or crediting the appropriate purchases or sales account. As to import purchases, the general cost definition seems applicable. The cost means the sum of the applicable expenditures and charges directly or indirectly incurred in bringing the article to its existing condition and location.[1] Fluctuations in exchange rates occur after the article is brought to its existing location. They have no effect on the article's condition. The exchange gain or loss is not a function of procurement; it is a finance function, a decision to accept or avoid the risk involved in delayed payment. As discussed previously, the risk can be managed through hedging. As a financial expense or revenue, the exchange gain or loss should not be charged directly to the foreign sales or purchases account.

FINANCIAL REPORTING OF FOREIGN TRADE ACCOUNT BALANCES

The Balance Sheet Valuation of Foreign Receivables and Payables

The general rule followed in the recording of foreign transactions is that each phase of a transaction is recorded at the prevailing exchange rate. The purchase or sale is recorded at the rate prevailing on the date of invoice or shipment. The payment on a subsequent date is recorded at the rate prevailing at that time. Any exchange gain or loss derived due to changes in the rate prevailing between the two dates is reported separately. When the time period between the purchase or sale date and payment date spans two periods, an allocation problem arises.

There are two dimensions to the allocation problem. First, the valuation of the foreign receivable or payable is necessary for proper balance sheet presentation. Secondly, the disposition of any exchange gain or loss must be properly reported.

The current practice concerning valuation of foreign receivables and payables is that foreign currency monetary balances are translated at the exchange rate prevailing on the balance sheet date. This is consistent with a two-transaction approach, which declares that the purchase or sale is a transaction separate from the settlement transaction.

The change in balance sheet valuation of a foreign receivable or payable may be recorded directly in the pertinent account. It can also be recorded in a separate accrual account or a contraaccount. Since the documents substantiating the balance sheet amount are in terms of the foreign currency, the most appropriate method is to record the change in domestic currency valuation directly in the accounts. Exhibits 3.1 and 3.2 compare the two methods; the accrual and contraaccount possibilities are shown as one method. Recording the valuation change directly in the pertinent receivable or payable account has the advantage of showing the present translated value which should be reported on the balance sheet.

EXHIBIT 3.1

Illustration of Foreign Sale

	Direct Charge to Account		Charge to Contraaccount or Accrual Account	
December 1				
Accounts receivable	11,150		11,150	
Sales		11,150		11,150
To record the sale of merchandise to a foreign company for LC 10,000, terms net/60 days; current exchange rate of LC 1.00 = U.S. $1.115.				
December 31				
Exchange gains and losses	30			
Accounts receivable		30		
or				
Exchange gains or losses			30	
Allowance for loss on foreign exchange				30
To adjust year-end balance to current exchange rate valuation of LC 1.00 = U.S. $1.112.				
January 30				
Foreign exchange	11,130		11,130	
Allowance for loss on foreign exchange			30	
Accounts receivable		11,120		11,150
Exchange gains and losses		10		10
To record receipt of LC 10,000 in payment of Dec. 1 invoice; current spot rate of LC 1.00 = U.S. $1.113.				

Source: Compiled by the author.

EXHIBIT 3.2

Illustration of Foreign Purchase

	Direct Charge to Account		Charge to Contraaccount or Accrual Account	
December 1				
Purchase	11,150		11,150	
Accounts payable		11,150		11,150
To record purchase of imported goods from a foreign merchant for LC 10,000, payable net/60 days.				
December 31				
Exchange gains and losses	10			
Accounts payable		10		
or				
Exchange gains and losses			10	
Accrued liability from loss on foreign exchange				10
To adjust year-end balance to current exchange rate valuation of LC 1.00 = U.S. $1.116.				
January 30				
Foreign exchange	11,170		11,170	
Cash		11,170		11,170
To record purchase of foreign exchange at rate of LC 1.00 = U.S. $1.117				
January 30				
Accounts payable	11,160		11,150	
Accrued liability from loss on foreign exchange			10	
Exchange gains and losses	10		10	
Foreign exchange		11,170		11,170
To record the payment of December 1 invoice with foreign exchange of LC 10,000.				

Source: Compiled by the author.

Recognition of Exchange Gains and Losses

The second dimension to the period allocation problem is the proper disposition of the recorded exchange gains and losses. Since the actual gain or loss is attributable to a financial management decision separate from the trade transaction, the gains or losses derived from valuation of the receivables or payables at the time of an exchange rate change are recognized as current operating gains and losses. As such the exchange gains and losses are reported on the income statement. If the amounts are material, disclosure of the amounts on the income statement may be necessary for a fair presentation.

FOREIGN INVESTMENTS

Investments in international ventures may take one of several forms. In accounting a distinction is made between two kinds of investment: temporary and permanent. Temporary investments take the nature of marketable securities; the securities are purchased from temporarily excessive cash. Such excess cash may derive from seasonal or cyclical movements of volume and working capital, or they may be accumulated for a future capital investment. Permanent or long-term investments may take the form of investments in branches, joint ventures, partnerships, or corporations. They are acquired with the intention of holding them for a number of years. Whereas short-term investments are classified as current assets, permanent investments are classified, in a separate category below the current asset section, as long-term investments or simply investments.

Foreign Marketable Securities

When a firm decides to acquire foreign marketable securities as an investment of excess cash, the firm has practically as many alternatives as for a domestic investment. Foreign common stock investments can be acquired through the registered stock exchanges in the United States. There are about 25 foreign stocks listed on the New York Stock Exchange and approximately 65 foreign stocks listed on the American Stock Exchange. If the security broker is a member of a foreign stock exchange such as the Toronto Stock Exchange, the leading Canadian exchange, the broker may purchase the securities for the corporation. Needless to say, the foreign securities also can be acquired privately and in the over-the-counter market.

Over-the-counter foreign securities may be represented by American depositary receipts (ADRs), representing ownership of securites physically deposited abroad. The ADRs are quoted in U.S. dollars and are valid only for securities supported by validation certificates showing proof of compliance with tax and ownership regulations.

Accounting for Temporary Foreign Investments

The accounting for temporary foreign investments follows the same principles used for domestic investments. Generally the cost-or-market rule applies for industrial firms which acquire the securities as an investment of idle cash. The costs of acquisition, including any interest equalization tax, are recorded as an asset. Costs paid in foreign currency are translated at the conversion rate in effect at the time of the acquisition.

Sales proceeds from foreign investments are recorded at the realized value. If the amount received is in foreign currency, the amount is translated at the conversion rate in effect at the time of the sale. Also, in determining market price in applying the cost-or-market rule, the foreign market price on the balance sheet date is translated at the rate of exchange prevailing on that date.

Foreign Direct Investment

Permanent or long-term foreign investments are negotiated with the intention of holding them for a period of years. A foreign direct investment may consist of capital transferred, an advance or loan, or the direct investor's share of the reinvested earnings of an affiliated foreign entity. A direct investor may own as much as 10 percent or more of the voting power, earnings, or capital of the foreign entity. The entity may be a corporation, partnership, or branch engaged in business in a foreign country. The amount of direct investment is dependent on both the history of direct investment policy of a firm and the economic development of the foreign country or the fiscal relationship of that country with the home country.

Recording Long-Term Foreign Investments

There are two principal methods of accounting for long-term investments: the cost method and the equity method. These methods are presented in Accounting Principles Board (APB) Opinion no. 18 (1971) and may be summarized as follows:

The cost method. An investor records an investment in the stock of an investee at cost, and recognizes as income dividends received that are distributed from net accumulated earnings of the investee after the date of acquisition by the investor. The net accumulated earnings of an investee subsequent to the date of investment are recognized by the investor only to the extent distributed by the investee as dividends. Dividends received in excess of earnings subsequent to the date of investment are considered a return of investment and are recorded as reductions of cost of the investment. A series of operating losses of an investee or other factors may indicate that a decrease in value of the investment has occurred.which is other than temporary and should accordingly be recognized.

The equity method. An investor initially records an investment in the stock of an investee at cost, and adjusts the carrying amount of the investment to recognize the investor's share of the earnings or losses of the investee after the date of acquisition. The amount of the adjustment is included in the determination of net income by the investor, and such amount reflects adjustment similar to those made in preparing consolidated statements including adjustment to eliminate intercompany gains and losses, and to amortize, if appropriate, any difference between investor cost and underlying equity in net assets of the investee at the date of investment. The investment is also adjusted to reflect the investor's share of changes in the investee's capital. Dividends received from an investee reduce the carrying amount of the investment. A series of operating losses of an investee or other factors may indicate that a decrease in value of the investment has occurred which is other than temporary and which should be recognized even though the decrease in value is in excess of what would otherwise be recognized by application of the equity method. The opinion is quite specific in extending these accounting principles to investments in common stock of all unconsolidated subsidiaries, foreign as well as domestic.

Neither of the two methods is a valid substitute for consolidation and should not be used to justify exclusion of a subsidiary when consolidation is otherwise appropriate. The equity method should be followed when the investor has the ability to exercise significant influence over operating and financial policies of an investee even though he holds 50 percent or less of the voting stock. In order to achieve a reasonable degree of uniformity, a significant degree of influence is presumed to exist when an investor holds 20 percent or more of the voting stock of the investee. Thus, the promulgated guidelines can be summarized as follows:

Less than 20 percent ownership: use the cost method for recording.
20 percent to 50 percent ownership: use the equity method for recording.
More than 50 percent ownership: consolidate the financial statements.

The consolidation and translation of foreign sibsidiary financial statements is discussed in the next chapter.

Foreign Joint Ventures

Joint ventures may be incorporated or unincorporated. APB Opinion no. 18 describes a corporate joint venture as follows:

"Corporate joint venture" refers to a corporation owned and operated by a small group of businesses (the joint venturers) as a separate and specific business or project for the mutual benefit of the members of the group. The purpose of a corporate joint venture frequently is to share risks and rewards in developing a new market, product or technology; to combine complementary technological knowledge; or to pool resources in developing production or other facilities. A corporate joint venture also usually provides an arrangement under which each joint venturer may participate, directly or indirectly, in the overall management of the joint venture. Joint venturers thus have an interest or relationship other than as passive investors. An entity which is a subsidiary of one of the joint venturers is not a corporate joint venture. The ownership of a corporate joint venture seldom changes, and its stock is usually not traded publicly. A minority public ownership, however, does not preclude a corporation from being a corporate joint venture.

The opinion further declares that the equity method should be utilized to account for investments in common stock of corporate joint ventures, whether foreign or domestic.

A joint venture may be established because a 50 percent ownership is the maximum that a particular foreign government would allow under its foreign investment laws. Joint ventures may be negotiated, too, because the parent company needs a strong, local partner. But there are some drawbacks in a strict 50-50 arrangement. Who, for example assumes final responsibility? What happens when there is a tie vote? To bypass such unique barriers, special arrangements are made. Among them are the using of two kinds of stock, the allowing of a small percentage of ownership in the hands of a friendly mediator, the establishing of a special bylaw which extends the management power to one of the venturers, or simply the awarding of a management contract.

SUMMARY

The primary mechanism for financing export transactions is the letter of credit. There are three main types of letters of credit—the cash letter of credit, the traveler's letter of credit, and the commercial letter of credit. The main types of commercial letters in use today are confirmed irrevocable straight credits of foreign banks, unconfirmed irrevocable credits of domestic banks, and irrevocable straight credits of foreign correspondent banks. Other financing instruments of significance are: the authority to purchase, utilized mainly by Far Eastern banks; and dollar drafts, which are used to finance a substantial volume of U.S. exports.

The customary freight shipment terms, FOB-shipping point and FOB-destination are used in foreign trade transactions, along with the terms C & F, and CIF. Sellers usually bear all risks and costs up to the designated title transfer point; export duties become the obligation of the buyer.

Foreign trade transactions may be billed in the local currency of the exporter or that of the importer. When the billing is in the trader's local currency, the trader has no foreign exchange risk. But for billings in foreign currencies, an exchange gain or loss may occur. The gain or loss derives when the exchange rate at the time of settlement is at variance with the rate at the time of the sale or purchase. Since the exchange gain or loss derivation is not a function of procurement or sales but of finance, it is recorded as a financial revenue or expense.

Receivables and payables are translated at the exchange rates prevalent at the balance sheet date. Any exchange gain or loss recorded before the final settlement is considered to be realized; the gains or losses are credited or charged to net income in the period of the rate change.

In accounting, foreign investments are treated in the same manner that domestic investments are. Short-term or temporary investments are classified as current assets and recorded by the application of the cost-or-market rule. Long-term or permanent investments are separately classified on the balance sheet and are reported by the use of the following guidelines:

Less than 20 percent ownership: use the cost method of accounting.
20 to 50 percent ownership: use the equity method of accounting.
More than 50 percent ownership: consolidate the financial statements.

Foreign securities may be acquired in the same market channels used in domestic securities. Some foreign securities in the over-the-counter market are represented by ADRs, which show proof of ownership of securities physically deposited abroad.

Long-term investments include capital advances or loans, or reinvested earnings in a foreign entity. The amount of such investments depends upon the firm's direct investment program as well as the status of the foreign country's economic development and fiscal relationship with the home country. Such investments may be subject to capital investment laws of the foreign country involved. Sometimes this may necessitate establishing a joint venture.

NOTE

1. American Institute of Certified Public Accountants, *Restatement and Revision of Accounting Research Bulletins*, Accounting Research Bulletin No. 43 (New York: AICPA, 1953), p. 28.

4

FASB #8

Foreign branch and subsidiary accounting is generally much the same as domestic branch and subsidiary accounting. The added international environmental complexities are the accounting problems arising from the currency differences. First, there is the financial accounting problem. If the accounting data of the foreign operations are to be incorporated into combined financial statements, the foreign currency data must be expressed in homogeneous monetary units—that is, in the currency of the home office. Second, there is the managerial accounting problem. Management is accustomed to thinking in terms of the home office currency; thus the foreign investment must be expressed in the home office currency in order to evaluate the return on the investment.

For a U.S. firm, financial statements of foreign operations may be translated at the company's headquarters or at the foreign operational level. If translation is performed in the United States, key figures are returned to management in the foreign countries. Also, various regular and special reports concerning foreign exchange are prepared in the United States and sent to the foreign managers.

Usually the foreign executives are rather autonomous in managing the foreign operations. Awareness of financial position and operational results is fostered by translating the financial statements before transmission to the United States. Even when the treasury function of exchange risk control is centralized, the reports in dollars are prepared locally for transmission to the U.S. headquarters. The translation into the language and currency of the parent company aids in communication of results and directives.

Though the foreign operations may be managed rather autonomously, the usual accounting assumption is that the foreign operations are considered to be extensions of the home country operations. The financial statement presentation is based on the pervasive accounting principle which dictates that the initial recordings of assets and liabilities be measured at exchange prices. The exchange rates prevailing at the time of each transaction must then be used to translate the transactions negotiated in a foreign currency. Because the times of the transactions are determinant in the recording process, the method of translation for foreign currency financial statements is called the temporal approach.

BALANCE SHEET ITEMS

Under the temporal approach, sometimes called the monetary-nonmonetary approach, balance sheet items which represent current values are translated at current, balance sheet date exchange rates, and items representing historical values are translated at the rate prevailing at the time of the transactions. A sample list of rates used to translate assets and liabilities is presented in Exhibit 4.1.

Foreign Monetary Assets and Liabilities

The principles for recording international financial items are the same as those used for recording domestic financial items. As indicated in the preceding chapter, the value of foreign receivables is translated at the rate prevailing at the balance sheet date. This is consistent with the principle of valuating at net realizable value.

In using the prevailing balance sheet rate for translating payables, liabilities are recorded at current liquidation value. Cash and other financial assets are also translated at the current rate. This assumes that these items are readily convertible into the home office currency. The underlying going-concern concept is involved in the application of these financial accounting principles.

Foreign Inventories

The accounting principles for foreign inventories remain the same as those in domestic operations. For example, if inventories are kept on a first-in-first-out (FIFO) cost basis in domestic operations, the FIFO cost basis should be used for the same type of merchandise sold through the foreign entity. The accounting, then, is used on a consistent basis.

In regard to foreign inventories, the Financial Accounting Standards Board (FASB) recommends the use of the cost-or-market rule. It is stated as follows:[1]

EXHIBIT 4.1

Rates Used to Translate Assets and Liabilities

	Translation Rates	
	Current	Historical
Assets		
Cash on hand and demand and time deposits	x	
Marketable equity securities		
Carried at cost		x
Carried at current market price	x	
Accounts and notes receivable and related unearned discount	x	
Allowance for doubtful accounts and notes receivable	x	
Inventories		
Carried at cost		x
Carried at current replacement price or current selling price	x	
Carried at net realizable value	x	
Carried at contract price (produced under fixed price contracts)	x	
Prepaid insurance, advertising, and rent		x
Refundable deposits	x	
Advances to unconsolidated subsidiaries	x	
Property, plant, and equipment		x
Accumulated depreciation of property, plant, and equipment		x
Cash surrender value of life insurance	x	
Patents, trademarks, licenses, and formulas		x
Goodwill		x
Other intangible assets		x
Liabilities		
Accounts and notes payable and overdrafts	x	
Accrued expenses payable	x	
Accrued losses on firm purchase commitments	x	
Refundable deposits	x	
Deferred income		x
Bonds payable or other long-term debt	x	
Unamortized premium or discount on bonds or notes payable	x	
Convertible bonds payable	x	
Accrued pension obligations	x	
Obligations under warranties	x	

Source: Financial Accounting Standards Board, *Accounting for the Translation of Foreign Currency Transactions and Foreign Currency Financial Statements*, Statement of Financial Accounting Standards, no. 8 (Stamford: FASB, October 1975), p. 20.

To apply the role of cost or market, whichever is lower, translated historical cost shall be compared with translated market. Application of the rule in dollars may require write-downs to market in the translated statements even though no write-down in the foreign statements is required by the rule. It may also require a write-down in the foreign statements to be reversed before translation if the translated market amount exceeds translated historical cost; the foreign currency cost shall then be translated at the historical rate. Once inventory has been written down to market in the translated statements, that dollar amount shall continue to be the carrying amount in the dollar financial statements until the inventory is sold or a further write-down is necessary.

There are two facets to the application of this principle. First, the original cost must be recorded and translated. Second, the market value must be computed and translated.

The merchandise sold through a foreign entity may be shipped to that entity from the headquarters or purchased locally by the entity. Because the purchase of resale merchandise abroad will require the acquisition of foreign exchange at the free market buying rate, the transfer of merchandise from the home office also should be at the free market buying rate prevailing at the time of the transfer. Exhibit 4.2 illustrates the two situations, assuming a 4:1 exchange rate.

If the inventory is still on hand at the end of a fiscal accounting period, the 4:1 rate would be used to translate the foreign inventory into U.S. dollars. The translated value of $250 (LC 1,000 ÷ 4) equals the original cost. But what if the exchange rate changes? If the year-end rate becomes 4.2:1, should the translated inventory value be changed to $238.10? Or, should the translated value be increased to $277.78 when the rate changes to 3.6:1? A strict cost interpretation would dictate the continued use of the 4:1 rate. To analyze the effects of the various rate changes, Exhibit 4.3 presents examples showing the gross profit if the total amount is sold for LC 2,000 in the following accounting period when the prevailing exchange rate is still at the year-end rate.

Under the cost basis, the gross profit constitutes the difference between the sales price translated at the rate prevailing at the date of sale and the original cost translated at the rate prevailing at the time of acquisition. Thus, any changes in the exchange rate are reflected directly in the gross profit. In some cases of foreign currency devaluations, this could mean a postponement of loss. For example, if the selling price is less than LC 1,050, there would be a negative gross profit. The cost-or-market rule then applies in translating foreign inventories.

If market, that is, currency replacement cost, remains the same in local currency, translating the acquisition cost at the balance sheet exchange rate would have the effect of reducing the inventory to the current replacement cost

EXHIBIT 4.2

Translation of Foreign Inventories

Illustration of Inventory Purchased Locally

Entries on Branch Records

Foreign exchange	LC 1,000	
Home office		LC 1,000

To record cable transfer from home office at current
cable transfer rate.

Inventory	LC 1,000	
Foreign exchange		LC 1,000

To record purchase of resale merchandise.

Entries on Home Office Records

Foreign branch	$250	
Cash		$250

To record cable transfer of funds to branch.

Illustration of Inventory Shipped from Home Office

Entry on Branch Records

Inventory	LC 1,000	
Home office		LC 1,000

To record receipt of merchandise shipment, costing $250
translated at current free market buying rate.

Entry on Home Office Records

Foreign branch	$250	
Inventory		$250

To record shipment of resale merchandise to branch.

Source: Compiled by the author.

EXHIBIT 4.3

Illustrative Effects of Exchange Rate Changes on Translated Inventory Cost

	Branch	Translated Value at Remittance Rates		
Income Statement	Records	4:1	4.2:1	3.6:1
Sales	LC 2,000	$500	$476.20	$555.56
Cost of goods sold	1,000	250	250.00	250.00
Gross profit	1,000	250	226.20	305.56
Balance sheet				
Cash (foreign exchange)	LC 2,000	$500	$476.20	$555.56
Home office	1,000	250	250.00	250.00
Gross profit	1,000	250	226.20	305.56

The entries to close the branch records and transfer the cash to the headquarters would be as follows:

Sales	LC 2,000		
Inventory (or cost of goods sold)		2,000	
Income summary		1,000	
To close the branch nominal accounts			
for the period.			

Income summary	LC 1,000		
Home office		1,000	
To close the income to the home office.			
Home office	LC 2,000		
Cash (foreign exchange)		2,000	
To record cable transfer of LC 2,000 to home			
office at prevailing rate of exchange.			

The entries to record the above information on the home office records under the three different remittance rates would be as follows:

	4:1	4.2:1	3.6:1
Foreign branch	$250	$226.20	$305.56
Net income of branch	$250	$226.20	$305.56
To record branch net income.			
Cash	500	476.20	555.56
Foreign branch	500	476.40	555.56
To record receipt of cash by cable transfer			
from branch.			

Source: Compiled by the author.

in dollars. For example, when the exchange rate declined from 4:1 to 4.2:1, the inventory would be valued at $238.10 (LC 1,000 ÷ 4.2). No entry should be made in the branch records. The entry on the home office records at the year-end would be as follows:

Exchange gains and losses	$11.90	
Foreign branch		$11.90
To record reduction of foreign inventory to		
current replacement cost.		

Where the exchange rate rose to 3.6:1, the historical cost would be used. Since the inventory would be $277.78 (LC 1,000 ÷ 3.6) at the current rate, the market value would be higher than cost. Translating at the historical rate of 4:1 would maintain the inventory at $250 on the home office records. A comparison of the three situations under these assumptions would be as follows:

	Branch Records	Translated Values		
		4:1 rate	4.2:1 rate	3.6:1 rate
Sales	LC 2,000	$500.00	$476.20	$555.56
Cost of goods sold	1,000	250.00	238.10	250.00
Gross profit	1,000	250.00	238.10	305.56

In the case of the write-down of the inventory to the 4.2:1 translation rate, the effect is to maintain the 50 percent normal gross profit rate in the year of sale. The exchange loss would be taken in the year the exchange rate dropped.

It may be considered desirable to continue to report the 50 percent normal gross profit also when the exchange rate rose. The year-end adjustment on the home office records would be:

Foreign branch	$27.78	
Unrealized exchange gain		$27.78
To adjust inventory to current replacement cost.		

The unrealized exchange gain is a deferred credit reported in the liability section of the balance sheet. Proper parenthetical or footnote disclosure would be necessary to indicate that the inventory of the foreign branch is reported at current replacement cost, which is higher than original cost. In the year of sale, the exchange gain would become realized and be reported on the income statement as other revenue.

In the above illustrations, the assumption was that the foreign selling price and replacement cost remained the same in the local currency. A more realistic assumption is that the market price also fluctuated in the foreign country. For example, if the replacement cost of the merchandise rose to LC 1,050 when the exchange rate dropped to 4.2:1, the original cost of $250 (LC 1,000 ÷4) is the same as the replacement cost of $250 (LC 1,050 ÷ 4.2). Provided the selling price also rose by 5 percent to LC 2,100, the dollar profit would be the same. However, the entries in the records would differ. If original cost is used, no entry would have to be made in the records. When the inventory is translated, the historical rate of 4:1 is used. But if the replacement cost is used, the branch office would have to record the inventory increase. The entry is as follows:

Inventory   LC 50
       Home office   LC 50
To record increase in inventory as
   credit to the home office.

The effect would be in the income statement of the branch.

The income statement of the branch under the two methods would appear as follows:

	Branch	Translated	Branch	Translated
Sales	LC 2,100	$500	LC 2,100	$500
Cost	1,000	250	1,050	250
Gross profit	1,100	250	1,050	250

The use of replacement cost has the advantage of showing the normal 50 percent profit margin on the branch statement.

If the replacement price in local currency did not rise as much as the exchange rate declined, the replacement cost would be less than the original cost; the rate of exchange prevailing on the balance sheet date should be used to translate the inventory. Similarly, if the local currency replacement price increased more than the exchange rate declined, the original cost would be lower than the replacement cost; the inventory should be translated at the historical exchange rate. Also, if the difference between the selling price percentage increase and the replacement price percentage increase is greater than the exchange rate percentage decline, the replacement price should be reduced only to net realizable value. Net realizable value is the selling price less a reasonable percentage to cover selling and local expenses.

Permanent Investments

For permanent investments accounted for under the equity method, the foreign statement balances also must be translated at the exchange rates appropriate for foreign branch or subsidiary operations.

Fixed Assets

The cost principle is the underlying concept in the recording of fixed assets. The fixed assets of a foreign entity may be recorded in the entity ledger or only in the home office ledger. If the records are kept in the entity ledger, the balance should be translated into dollars at the exchange rates current when the assets were acquired.

In order to translate the long-term asset balances at historical rates, the acquisition dates must be known. This entails additional subsidiary records. Rather than keeping records of all acquisition dates, the acquisitions are often grouped into years. A representative exchange rate is then applied to all acquisitions of each year. Another method is to maintain dual currency accounts showing the acquisition cost in both U.S. dollars and local currency.

Depreciation Allowances

As noted in Exhibit 4.1, the depreciation on foreign fixed assets is computed on the original cost as stated in U.S. dollars. This method is designed to ensure adequate charges to cover equivalent dollar cost in cases of later devaluation or decline in the exchange rate.

Asset Retirements

Since the original cost and the related accumulated depreciation account are translated at historical rates, the elimination of retired fixed assets must be at the same rate. However, if proceeds are received in salvaging the assets, the proceeds must be translated at the rate prevailing at the time of sale. This may mean that a loss in local currency is a gain in dollars or vice versa. For example, assume a machine with a book value of LC 1,000, acquired when the exchange rate was 4:1, was sold for LC 1,200 when the exchange rate was 5:1. The results would be as follows:

	Local Currency	Rate	U.S. Currency
Proceeds on disposal	LC 1,200	.20	$240
Book value of asset	1,000	.25	250
Gain (loss) on sale	200		(10)

Companies with assets invested in countries with declining exchange rates must be aware of and budget for the erosion of such assets.

Intangibles and Prepaid Expenses

Since the cost principle is generally applicable to intangible assets and to prepaid expenses, the rules applicable to fixed assets apply to these assets as well. Amortization and depletion charges also are based on the original cost in dollars.

INCOME STATEMENT ACCOUNTS

The cost principle and the going-concern concept also apply in the translation of income statement accounts. As indicated above, the depreciation, depletion, and amortization charges are based on the original cost in dollars. Revenues and other expenses also should be based on the rates prevailing at the time of each transaction. However, in many cases, the large volume of transactions involved makes the practical application of this principle rather difficult. Thus, short cuts through the use of average rates are devised to derive fairly accurate approximations. Specifically, the FASB position is as follows:[2]

> Revenue and expense transactions shall be translated in a manner that produces approximately the same dollar amounts that would have resulted had the underlying transactions been translated into dollars on the dates they occurred. Since separate translation of each transaction is usually impractical, the specified result can be achieved by using an average rate for the period. However, revenue and expenses that relate to assets and liabilities translated at historical rates shall be translated at the historical rates used to translate the related assets or liabilities.

When the exchange rate does not fluctuate during the year, translating the accumulated totals at closing rates will produce the same result as in the individual translation of each transaction. To be consistent, however, items charged to revenues or expense from previous periods must be translated at historical rates. The items translated at historical rates will depend on the time of original recording of the balance sheet items. When the exchange rate fluctuates during the year, the closing rate translation may yield results which would vary from the rates prevailing during the year. In practice various rates are applied.

Month-end Closing Rates

Month-end closing rates are often used to determine the average rate. This may be accomplished in two ways. One method is to apply the year's average rate to the year's accumulations of revenue and costs. Under the latter method, a weighted average may be necessary if the revenues and/or costs are seasonal or sporadic.

Monthly Average Rates

The month-end closing rate is particularly applicable when the exchange rate is stable or has shown only minor fluctuations. Under such conditions, the closing rate is preferred because of its simplicity in computation and clerical application. If the closing rate does not satisfactorily represent the rates prevailing during the month, an average rate applicable to each month must be computed. This may be a simple average of the daily rates. When the volume of transactions tends to be rather steady throughout the period and the exchange rates tend to be evenly dispersed around the average, the simple average rate is the most representative.

The simple average is determined by adding each day's average of the high and low rates of exchange for the period and dividing this sum by the number of days making the total. As in the application of the month-end closing rates, the monthly average rates may be applied in two principal ways. First, the average of daily rates may be applied to the applicable month's accumulated revenues and costs. The resultant dollar figures for each month are added together to determine the dollar totals for the period. When exchange rates and volume tend to fluctuate appreciably from month to month, this procedure is preferred. The result is a weighted monthly average. Second, the unweighted monthly average is merely the sum of the monthly average rates in the period divided by the number of months in the period. This average is then applied to the accumulated totals of the revenue and costs for the period. When the rate movement and transaction volume tend to be steady, this average rate would be quite representative.

Standard Current Rates

For some stable currencies, the market rates merely oscillate around a pegged rate. To make minor adjustments for small fluctuations may be confusing to management. Furthermore, it adds to computational costs. Many companies then use a standard rate throughout the year.

The rate may be the pegged rate, or in the case of the Canadian dollar, the par. If necessary, the rate may be rounded off to the nearest cent. Such bookkeeping rates are reviewed regularly but would not be adjusted unless clearly inappropriate. At the year-end, the closing rate, which may also be rounded off to the nearest whole unit, is computed. If applicable, this rate becomes the standard rate for the following year.

Remittance Rates

Dividends are translated at the rate at which the foreign currency remittance is realized in dollars. Very occasionally, such remittance rates are used as the rate of translating current revenue and costs of foreign operations.

Historical Rates

The historical rate is universally used to translate current charges for depreciation, depletion, and amortization. This is necessary to cover equivalent dollar cost determined at the date of acquisition. The historical rate is determined and applied in the same manner as the rate used to translate the related asset account. This also applies to prepaid expenses which are translated at historical rates at the year-end.

The historical rate may be used on the balance sheet date for inventories shown at historical cost. In such instances, the same historical rate must be utilized in the translation of that portion of the cost of goods sold in the subsequent period.

Penalty Rates

In some cases, certain imports of inventories or fixed assets are taxed by requiring that the import be paid at exchange rates higher than the free market rate. In these instances, the difference between the free market rate and the penalty rate is charged to the related inventory or fixed asset item. Such charges are equivalent to transportation or installation costs.

Preferential Rates

Some countries encourage essential or desirable dollar imports into the local economy by allowing a favorable rate of exchange for purchase of dollars to settle the payments for the imports. Such favorable rates on imported products act as a form of government subsidy designed to maintain lower selling prices to the local consumer.

Inventories and liabilities derived from such special imports must be translated at the preferential exchange rates. However, unless the liability and the related asset at the preferential rates are matched in amounts, debit or credit balances may arise in the translation into dollars. Such debit or credit balances would be erroneous exchange losses or gains. There are two methods by which such errors are avoided.[3]

One method, called the matching technique, is to continue, in translations, to match the assets and liabilities connected with the preferential rate. If the liability is paid before the related asset is disposed of, only that asset portion equivalent to the liability outstanding is translated at the preferential rate.

The other procedure, called the deferred accounting technique, is to set up deferred charges or credits in the balance sheet. In translation, if the asset acquired at preferential rates is less than the related liability still existing, a deferred charge would be established. If the dollar component of the inventory exceeds the related debt, an additional deferred credit must be established.

SUMMARY

The added international environmental complexities in accounting for foreign branch operations arise from currency differences. For financial accounting purposes, the accounting data must be expressed in homogeneous monetary units—that is, in the same currency. For management use, the financial statements must be expressed in the currency in which management is accustomed to thinking.

The accounting principles for foreign operations are the same as for domestic operations. Financial items are valued at their net realizable value. Inventories are recorded at cost, or by using the cost-or-market rule. Fixed assets, permanent investments, intangible assets, deferred charges, and the related depreciation and amortization charges are based on historical cost. Revenue and expenses other than depreciation and amortization charges are recorded at the negotiated exchange prices.

In recording foreign operations, the exchange rates prevailing at the time of the relevant transaction are appropriate and applicable. However, for practical purposes, the income statement accounts are often recorded through the use of average rates. For these accounts, the best method is to translate each month's transactions at the appropriate average rate and then add the translated amounts to the previously translated accumulated amounts.

NOTES

1. Financial Accounting Standards Board, *Accounting for the Translation of Foreign Currency Transactions and Foreign Currency Financial Statements*, Statement of Financial Accounting Standards, no. 8 (Stamford: FASB, October 1975), pp. 22-23. See also, C. Willard Elliott, "The Lower-of-Cost-and-Market Test for Foreign Inventories," *N.A.A. Bulletin* 46, no. 6 (February 1965): 12-17.

2. Ibid., p. 6.

3. National Association of Accountants, *Management Accounting Problems in Foreign Operations*, N.A.A. Research Report 36 (New York: NAA, 1960), pp. 47-55.

INTERNATIONAL TAXES

A general familiarity with the taxes involved in international transactions is a necessity for the accountant working in the international sphere. The international management accountant, unless he is a tax expert, does not have to know all the technical aspects of international taxation, but should be able to handle tax problems in accounting for foreign currency transactions, for foreign investments, and for intercorporate transfers.

The discussion of tax considerations in this chapter is from the U.S. viewpoint. Some consideration will be given to the tax systems and problems involved with accounting for international operations. The emphasis is on the accounting for the taxes rather than on detailed explanations of the intricacies involved in the technical aspects of international taxation.

FOREIGN CURRENCY TRANSACTIONS

Foreign Trade

There is no international tax accounting problem for U.S. importers or exporters that purchase or sell goods or services billed in the home currency. Foreign currency fluctuations have no effect on the transaction since the settlement will be in the home country currency.

There also is no international tax problem when a firm purchases or sells goods or services, and bills in a foreign currency which is settled at time of delivery. Since the trade transaction and the settlement transaction occur at the same time, no exchange gain or loss will occur. An exchange gain or loss may arise, however, if the currency conversion does not coincide with the trade transaction, since the trade and the settlement are considered to be two different transactions.

The two-transaction approach dictates that a gain or loss occurs on a foreign currency monetary balance when an exchange rate changes. The exchange gains and losses may be reported as taxable income or loss in the period in which the exchange rate changes. However, the provisions of income tax regulations in the United States would appear to allow the recognition of the exchange gain or loss at the time of the final settlement of an open balance. Recognition of the gain or loss at settlement date may present a tax allocation problem.

Since the two-transaction approach is used for accounting purposes, the exchange gains and losses are recorded at the time of an exchange rate change. If for income tax purposes, the tax on the gain or loss is not recorded until the time of the settlement of the transaction, a timing difference results. Tax allocation accounting would require recording the tax at the time that the exchange gain or loss is recorded. If the payment is not made until later, a deferred tax balance must be established. Since the difference between the dates of the trade transaction and the settlement transaction is usually less than six months, the exchange gains or losses are normally taxable at ordinary tax rates.

Forward Exchange Contracts

The two-transaction approach applies as well to forward exchange contract transactions. Generally, the gain or loss on hedging transactions becomes taxable at the time of an exchange rate change.

A key question in the recording of the tax aspects of forward contracts is whether or not a gain or loss is a short-term ordinary income item, or a long-term capital item. In the United States when a forward exchange transaction is used to hedge against a foreign exchange risk in the dollar value of foreign capital assets—for example, the stock of a foreign subsidiary—the exchange gain or loss is categorized as a capital item. If the forward exchange contract is undertaken to hedge a normal export or import transaction, the exchange gain or loss is an ordinary income item.*

---

*An interpretation of Section 1233 of the Internal Revenue Code would indicate that unless there is an actual transfer of title of a forward contract by selling or assigning it to a third party, no sale or exchange is considered to have taken place for tax purposes. Thus, all exchange gains and losses on forward contracts, unless they are otherwise sold or assigned, are considered to be ordinary gains and losses.

Foreign Currency Loans

Since foreign exchange is considered to be a monetary asset rather than a commodity, exchange gains and losses are taxed when a foreign exchange loan is repaid. Two points are considered to be relevant in this case. First, the difference in timing between the recording of the exchange gain or loss for accounting purposes and the recording for tax purposes calls for tax allocation accounting. Secondly, whether an exchange gain or loss on a foreign currency loan is taxable as a capital gain or loss or as an ordinary income or loss is determined not by the length of the loan but in accordance with the purpose for which the loan is obtained. In other words if the loan is for a routine sales or purchase transaction, the gain or loss is taxable as an ordinary item. If the loan takes the form of a long-term note, bond, or other debt instrument used to finance a capital asset, the gain or loss may be treated as if it is received from the sale of a capital asset.*

FOREIGN INVESTMENTS

Foreign Marketable Securities

In investments in foreign marketable stocks and bonds, four different tax problems arise. They include the accounting for taxes involved in the acquisition of the securities, the tax accounting upon the receipt of dividends, the tax problems involved in the revaluation of the securities on a specific balance sheet date, and the accounting for taxes upon the final disposition of the marketable security.

Excise taxes, for example, assessed at the time of the acquisition of marketable security become part of the cost of acquiring the investment. An independently paid tax, such as an interest equalization tax, is recorded as part of the cost of the investment.

Upon receipt of cash dividends or interest on a marketable security, the revenue is taxed in the period of receipt. However, some foreign jurisdictions require a withholding tax on dividend distributions. In such cases, the amount of the foreign tax which does not exceed the normal amount of tax to be paid in the United States can be used as a credit against the federal income tax liability. Therefore, the receipt of a dividend in which a foreign tax has been withheld must be recorded at the gross amount. The difference between the gross amount and the cash received is then recorded as a claim against the U.S. taxes.

---

*Section 1232 of the Internal Revenue Code applies.

For companies that follow the cost-or-market rule for accounting purposes, market value is determined by using the exchange rate prevailing at the balance sheet date of determination. In this manner an exchange rate gain or loss is intermingled with the intrinsic gain or loss on the investment. Upon final sale of a security, the total loss is a taxable loss. Therefore, when a security is written down to a value lower than the cost, a relevant tax provision must be recorded. This constitutes a timing difference which requires tax allocation accounting. Tax allocation also may be required for companies that value their securities at market, as required by practice in specific industries.

Upon final disposition of a marketable security, the difference between the proceeds and the original cost is the realized taxable gain or loss. Any transaction taxes that are paid on the sale of the security serve to reduce the amount of the cash proceeds. If deferred tax balances have been established because the carrying amount of the marketable security had been adjusted to a market value, the deferred debits or credits are considered to be realized. The actual tax liability will be recorded upon the sale of the investment.

Foreign Direct Investments

Direct investments in foreign affiliates and joint ventures require two major considerations in addition to those involved in investments in foreign marketable securities. One is the tax allocation problem involved in the use of the equity method of accounting for investments. The other is the problem of accounting for the tax incentives which may be granted for certain types of investments in certain countries.

When earnings are recorded under the equity method of accounting for investments in affiliates or joint ventures, a timing difference occurs when the tax is accrued on the earnings but is not payable until dividends are received. The accrual of taxes and the tax rates applicable depend upon the firm's anticipation of the eventual disposition of the earnings of the affiliate or joint venture. If the earnings are expected to be realized by dividends, ordinary income rates apply. If the earnings are expected to be retained in the affiliate until final sale or disposition, capital gains rates apply.

Tax incentives in the form of direct government grants or tax credits may be recorded in several ways. The method depends upon the view taken as to the substance of the tax incentive. The amount of the tax incentive could be recorded as (1) a credit to contributed capital; (2) a reduction of the cost of the related fixed assets; (3) a credit to deferred income to be offset against assumed higher operating costs of future periods; or (4) a credit to the amount of income tax expense applicable to the income for the year in which the credit arises.

The availability of a grant or tax credit may be the determining influence in the decision to acquire a particular investment. Then, the appropriate entry is to record the investment grant or credit as a direct reduction of the acquisition cost or as a deferred credit to be amortized over the useful life of the related asset. An assumption of direct relationship would seem to be the most realistic.

If an investment grant or credit is considered to be a windfall profit with no contribution to income in any subsequent period, the amount of the grant or credit could be transferred directly to the income in the period in which the grant or credit is received. On the other hand, one could also argue that such a grant is a contribution other than from a shareholder and it thus should be credited directly to the shareholders' equity account. Crediting to the shareholders' equity account would assume also that the availability of the grant or credit is not a determining influence in the acquisition of the investment and that it provides no contribution to income in the current or later periods.

Investments in Foreign Branches

If branch records are maintained in the home office currency, there is no problem in determining the foreign source income for tax purposes. Under a procedure called the transaction method, each foreign currency transaction is translated at the time the transaction occurs.

Similar to the transaction approach is the temporal approch for translating foreign branch financial statements. This approach is also called the net worth or balance sheet method.[1] It is the same method used for translating the financial statements of a foreign subsidiary.

Another method, called the profit-and-loss or net income method, also has been used. Under this method, currently remitted profits are translated at the conversion rate prevailing at the date of the remittance. Depreciation and amortization items are translated at the historical rates of exchange applicable to the underlying assets. The remaining profit is translated at the year-end rate. No exchange gain or loss due to holding of foreign monetary assets is reported until the actual repatriation of the capital. This procedure also is used sometimes for determining the recorded income of affiliates which are accounted for under the equity method.

Controlled Foreign Corporations

Generally the financial statements of foreign subsidiaries may not be consolidated with those of domestic subsidiaries on the U.S. tax return. The foreign subsidiary income is taxable when the dividend is paid by the subsidiary to its parent company. The exchange rate used is the rate prevailing on the date of payment. The parent company is entitled to a foreign tax credit for a portion of the taxes paid by the subsidiary. The credit is against its parent company income tax. The purpose of the foreign tax credit is to avoid the possibility of a double taxation on the income.

To be sure that all income is taxed at its source, specified income of certain controlled foreign corporations may be taxable. According to the Revenue Act of 1962, controlled subsidiaries deriving more than 30 percent of the foreign subsidiary income from commissions, service, rentals, and product sales may have taxable income. Exceptions are provided for income from material manufactured by the controlled foreign subsidiary; the portion of profits from sales, consumption or disposition inside the country of incorporation of material purchased from a related company for resale without further reprocessing; for profits resulting from material purchased from an unrelated company for resale without further processing; and for the portion of profits from the sales outside the country of incorporation to unrelated persons. It is necessary to segregate the income of the controlled foreign subsidiary in order to determine the exact taxability of the foreign source income. Normally, the foreign financial statements will be translated under the temporal approach.

There are other specific tax provisions which may be applicable in determining taxable income. Generally, the geographical source of income is an important consideration for domestic and foreign corporations. More specifically, the segregation of the income according to geographical source may be very important in the proper determination of the foreign tax credit.[2]

The foreign tax credit may be taken only up to the amount of equivalent U.S. income tax liability, whether or not the tax is paid directly by the parent company or indirectly by the subsidiary. In certain cases, particularly for subsidiaries located in less developed countries, the credits derived from the income tax paid to all foreign countries may be totaled in determining the amount of the credit allowable against the U.S. income tax liability. The totaling of all foreign taxes paid into one tax credit amount is called the overall method. The overall method is beneficial when income is received from one or more high-tax countries as well as one or more low-tax countries. However, since the overall method requires the inclusion of losses, a careful analysis may be necessary. In other words, a certain amount of tax planning is necessary where there are a number of foreign subsidiaries.

OTHER INTERCORPORATE TAX CONSIDERATIONS

Intercompany Transfers

Tax planning is necessary because the tax burden can be shifted among countries according to transfer prices and the channeling of products and services. The planning may require some knowledge of the tax systems in other countries. There should be a knowledge of the difference in types of taxes, as well as of tax rates and tax bases. The types of taxes include sales taxes, purchase taxes, and value-added taxes as well as income taxes. Tax rates vary for special capital gains or losses, because of specific tax exemptions, and for border taxes.[3]

Executive Compensation Abroad

A type of exemption that is applicable in a transfer occurs when a U.S. citizen is employed by a foreign subsidiary. A U.S. citizen abroad for an 18-month period may exempt income up to $20,000 for the first three years of foreign residence and $25,000 for each full year thereafter. Of course, the amount depends upon the nature of the earned income. The exemption applies primarily to personal services income such as wages, commissions, and professional fees.

Special Corporations

Other specific provisions relating to international activities concern tax incentives offered through the establishment of special corporations. For example, there is the Western Hemisphere Trade Corporation, which is allowed a special tax rate for actively locating in the less developed areas of the American continent and nearby islands. Tax incentives are similarly extended to corporations trading in a possession of the United States, to domestic international sales corporations (DISCS) engaged in exporting of U.S.-produced goods, to export trade corporations established before the DISC provisions were enacted, and to specific country corporations operating in less developed countries.

Tax Allocation Problems

Already mentioned as problems that must be considered in accounting are the tax deferral techniques required where timing differences occur in recording of exchange gains and losses on forward contracts, and on undistributed earnings of affiliates. Other problems may be involved, such as the recognition of exchange gains and losses in the translation process within foreign subsidiaries which become taxable locally. In any case, the accountant involved in international transactions must be aware of the accounting as well as tax problems. The gathering of tax information for the tax planning program must be integrated into the company's total information system.

THE TAX PLANNING PROGRAM

Establishing the Program

In the establishment of the tax planning program, a statement of objectives is a necessary starting point.[4] In a multinational firm, the statement of objectives would probably dictate an equitable distribution of tax funds. Information requirements can then be established in the total information system of the firm in order to fulfill the tax objectives. The tax aspects of the information system include identification of the problems where taxes become an element of a key decision, such as the use of special corporations; the alternatives of various tax incentives including accelerated depreciation; and a possible minimum dividend distribution plan. Furthermore, the information system should provide management with a cognizance of major tax changes not only in the home country, but in the countries of foreign operations.

Administering the Program

The administration of the program requires an assignment of responsibility for the decision-making process, verification of the tax decisions, and a final evaluation of the tax program. Within the decision-making process, the controllers of the various subsidiaries may be required to submit tax projections. These along with the data provided from the information system will aid in the proper decision making under the tax planning program.

Once the tax planning program decisions have been established and are carried out, verification may be necessary. Thus, interaction between the tax consultants and the decision makers may be necessary to assure the proper carrying out of the tax planning. Furthermore, all tax returns from the various subsidiaries must be centrally reviewed for the proper amount of foreign tax credits, the proper payment of taxes, and even the possibility of contesting unjustified tax assessments.

Finally, an evaluation of the tax planning program is required to fulfill the goal of the total tax planning process. One key test is the analysis of the variance between the effective tax rate and the actual average rate for the various subsidiaries as well as in total. Finally, it is necessary to note any timing difference so that the proper deferred tax accounting is used.

NOTES

1. Business International, *Solving Accounting Problems for Worldwide Operations* New York: Business International, 1974), pp. 66-70.

2. Internal Revenue Service, *Foreign Tax Credit for U.S. Citizens and Resident Aliens*. Publication 514 (Washington, D.C.: U.S. Government Printing Office, 1975).

3. George Scott, *An Introduction to Financial Control and Reporting in Multinational Enterprises* (Austin: Bureau of Business Research, University of Texas, 1973).

4. Ibid., pp. 55-57. See also Ernest K. Briner, "International Tax Management," *Management Accounting* 54, no. 8 (February 1973): 47-50; and Edward L. Farrell, "Tax Planning and the Multinational Corporation," *Tax Planning*, February 1974, pp. 11-15.

III

MULTINATIONAL ENTERPRISE ACCOUNTING CONTROL

CHAPTER

6

MULTINATIONAL WORKING
CAPITAL MANAGEMENT

Multinational enterprise control consists of the stewardship of global investments for an optimized return. It includes the management of the international working capital, assuring its protection against exchange risk. The working capital management is further linked to international investment decision making and multinational transfer administration, and is integrated into the global information system of the firm.

Working capital management involves the international management of cash movements, the temporary investment of idle cash, the control of inventories and trade receivables, and the direction of trade payables and other current liabilities including tax obligations. Such management is complex in any business and must be handled in a systematic manner.

In the international environment, the flow of working capital is affected by inflation, remittance restrictions, exchange rate fluctuations, and business practices and government regulations that are culturally different from those of the home country. The immediate results of working capital management decisions can be viewed by the size of the exchange gains and losses. The amount of the exchange gain or loss depends on the firm's definition of exchange risk exposure. Though there may be different international views as to its definition, the most common approach presented herein coincides with the temporal approach to translation of foreign currency working capital.

EXCHANGE EXPOSURE ANALYSIS

The exchange exposure in a foreign currency is the amount of net financial assets in that currency. Inventories may or may not be included with the financial assets. To differentiate between inventory inclusion and addition, exposure may be broken down into minimum exposure excluding inventories and maximum exposure including inventories.[1]

Alternatively, exchange exposure can be presented inversely. That is, maximum exposure can be defined as net foreign assets less net foreign fixed and intangible assets. Minimum exposure is the maximum exposure less the inventories.

In order to determine the foreign exchange exposure in a particular currency, it is necessary to separate the dollar items and the other currency items on the local currency balance sheet. Exhibit 6.1 shows the balance sheet with the separation of nonlocal currency items, and the two methods of calculating exchange exposure. Since prepaid expenses reduce the cash exposed, they are not included in the computation of exchange exposure. Besides showing the exposure to foreign exchange risk, further schedules showing the amounts of assets covered by forward exchange contracts may be presented. Also, daily records of quoted exchange rates may be charted. Such charts also help in determining the rates to be used in translating financial statements.

Analysis of Exchange Gains and Losses

The analysis of gains and losses on foreign exchange may be performed in connection with the income statement or the funds flow statement. The income statement approach may be presented by a separate analysis statement or by an integrated income statement.

To illustrate the three approaches, Exhibit 6.2 presents hypothetical balance sheets at the beginning and end of the year along with the accompanying income statement. It shows the foreign subsidiary amounts in local currency and translated into dollars. The translation rates are indicated. Without a breakdown of the exchange gain or loss, the balance sheet in dollars must be plugged for the amount of net income in dollars. On the income statement, the plugged figure is the exchange gain or loss.

The Separate Statement of Analysis of Exchange Gain or Loss

In Exhibit 6.3, a separate statement of analysis is shown.[2] The statement commences with the breakdown of financial assets. This includes long-term financial debt and excludes physical assets including inventories. In this illustration, the net financial assets amount is a negative figure. Thus, a gain occurs as a result of the decline in the exchange rate.

The statement then proceeds to show the effects of other balance sheet items. The decline in the historical exchange rate for inventories shows an exchange loss. Since fixed assets continue to be translated at the same historical

EXHIBIT 6.1

The Elements of Exchange Exposure

Balance Sheet Breakdown

	Local Currency	Dollars	Other Currencies (in dollars)
Cash	10,000		
Foreign exchange		2,500	300
Receivables	12,000		
Inventories	13,000		
Fixed assets less accumulated depreciation	20,000		
Total assets	90,000	2,500	300
Current liabilities and accruals	20,000		
Long-term liabilities	10,000		
Due home office		1,000	
Total liabilities	30,000	1,000	
Net assets	60,000	1,500	300

Statement of Exchange Exposure

	Local Currency	Other Foreign Currencies (in dollars)
Cash	10,000	
Receivables	25,000	
Financial assets	35,000	300
Less		
Current liabilities	20,000	
Long-term liabilities	10,000	
Financial liabilities	30,000	
Minimum exposure (net financial assets)	5,000	300
Plus		
Inventories	35,000	
Maximum exposure	40,000	300
Net assets	60,000	300
Less net fixed assets	20,000	
Maximum exposure	40,000	300
Less inventories	35,000	
Minimum exposure	5,000	300

Source: Compiled by the author.

EXHIBIT 6.2

Illustrative Financial Statements with Plugged Exchange Adjustment

Balance Sheet, January 1

	Local Currency	Translation Rate[a]	Dollars
Cash	10,000	.25b	2,500
Receivables	20,000	.25b	5,000
Inventories	30,000	.27c	8,100
Fixed assets	50,000	.30c	14,000
Accumulated depreciation	(15,000)	.30c	(4,500)
Total assets	95,000		26,100
Current liabilities	25,000	.25b	6,250
Long-term loan	20,000	.25b	5,000
Capital stock	20,000	.30c	6,000
Retained earnings	30,000		8,850
Total liabilities and equity	95,000		26,100

Balance Sheet, December 31

	Local Currency	Translation Rate[a]	Dollars
Cash	10,000	.20b	2,000
Receivables	25,000	.20b	5,000
Inventories	35,000	.22c	7,700
Fixed assets: previous	50,000	.30c	15,000
additions	10,000	.21c	2,100
Accumulated depreciation	(20,000)	.30c	(6,000)
Total assets	110,000		25,800
Current liabilities	25,000	.20b	5,000
Long-term loan	20,000	.20b	4,000
Capital stock: previous	20,000	.30c	6,000
additions	10,000	.25c	2,500
Retained earnings			
Balance, January 1	30,000		8,850
Net income	10,000	.22d	550
Dividends paid	(5,000)		(1,100)
Total liabilities and equity	110,000		12,800

Income Statement for Year

	Local Currency	Exchange Rate*	Dollars
Sales	100,000	.23a	23,000
Cost of goods sold			
Inventory, January 1	30,000	.27c	8,100
Purchases	60,000	.23a	13,800
Inventory, December 31	(35,000)	.22c	(7,700)
Cost of goods sold	55,000		14,200
Gross profit	45,000		8,800
Wages and expenses	30,000	.23a	6,900
Depreciation	5,000	.30c	1,500
Total expenses	35,000		8,400
Income from operations	10,000		400
Exchange gains			150
Net income	10,000		550

a Average rate.
b Closing rate.
c Historical rate.
d Remittance rate.

Note: The beginning balance of the retained earnings in translated dollars is the balance as computed at the previous year end. The ending balance of retained earnings and the net income amount are the amounts derived—that is, plugged—in order to force the dollar balance sheet to balance. On the income statement, the exchange gain or loss is derived, or plugged, in order to force the income statement to show the amount of derived net income.

Source: Compiled by the author.

EXHIBIT 6.3

Illustrative Statement Showing Analysis of
Gain on Foreign Exchange for Year

	Local Currency	Analysis in Dollars
Cash	10,000	
Receivables	20,000	
Current liabilities	(25,000)	
Long-term loan	(20,000)	
Net financial assets	(15,000)	
Gain from change in rate from .25 to .20		750
Loss on inventory held during year, 30,000 X .05 (.27 – .22)		(1,500)
Difference between local currency profit plus depreciation (cash flow) translated at year-end rate of .20 and the similar dollars in the income statement		
Profit	10,000	400
Depreciation	5,000	1,500
Total per income statement	15,000	1,900
Translated at closing rate		3,000
Gain		1,100
Reduction of losses by investment prior to year-end		
Inventory increase, LC 5,000 @ .22 compared with .20	(5,000)	100
Fixed asset increase, LC 10,000 @ .21 compared with .20	(10,000)	100
Dividend remittance, LC 5,000 @ .22 compared with .20	(5,000)	100
Increase of loss due to capital stock issue prior to year-end, LC 10,000 @ .25 compared with .20	10,000	(500)
Closing balance—net financial assets	(10,000)	150
Cash	10,000	
Receivables	25,000	
Current liabilities	(25,000)	
Long-term loan	(20,000)	
Total	(10,000)	

Source: Compiled by the author.

rates, there is no exchange loss on their holding. The related depreciation is also translated at the historical rate. The local currency and dollar amount of depreciation must be added back to net income to derive the cash flow. There is a gain from the cash flow because the revenue translation rate is lower than the translation rates for costs and expenses. The gain derives from the recovery of costs and expenses at favorable rates.

Other balance sheet changes show the investments or disinvestments and their effect on the exchange position. Investments in inventories and fixed assets at rates more favorable than the closing rate show gains. Also, the remittance of dividends to the parent company at a favorable rate shows a gain. In contrast, the issue of capital stock adds to financial assets. With the decline in exchange rates following the capital stock issue, an exchange loss derives.

Finally, the summation of funds inflow and outflow with the beginning net financial assets gives the amount representing the ending net financial assets. This is verified with the accompanying schedule of individual financial assets and liabilities. In the summation, the exchange gains and losses are netted to arrive at the amount which agrees with the figure plugged on the income statement.

The Integrated Income Statement

Another method of showing the exchange gain and loss analysis is to present it as part of the income statement, as illustrated in Exhibit 6.4. This method has the advantage of showing the complete breakdown of the exchange gain or loss in the income statement.[3] The final dollar net income amount is then the figure reported on the retained earnings statement.

The exchange gain and loss breakdown is computed on the sources of balance sheet changes. Net income, capital stock issues, dividend remittances, depreciation or appreciation of the translated value of beginning net assets, and changes in the physical assets all reflect in exchange gains or losses. The analysis is similar to that shown in the separate statement; however, no correlation with the flow of net financial assets is presented.

The Integrated Funds Statement

A simplified, more easily readable method for showing the breakdown of exchange gains and losses is to prepare a multicolumn funds statement; Exhibit 6.5 shows the format. First, the local currency figures are translated at the proper prevailing rate. The local currency figures are again translated into dollars, but the closing rate is used for all amounts. The dollar gain and loss amounts shown represent the differences between the translated historical amounts and translated closing amounts.

EXHIBIT 6.4

Illustrative Income Statement Showing Exchange Gain Analysis

	Local Currency	Exchange Rate or Dollar Amounts	Dollars
Sales	100,000	.23[a]	23,000
Cost of goods sold			
Inventory, January 1	30,000	.27[b]	8,100
Purchases	60,000	.23[a]	13,800
Inventory, December 31	(35,000)	.22[b]	(7,700)
	55,000		14,200
Gross profit	45,000		8,800
Wages and expenses	30,000	.23[a]	6,900
Depreciation	5,000	.30[b]	1,500
	35,000		8,400
Income from operations	10,000		400
Exchange gain and loss on net income			
As computed above		400	
At year-end rate (.20)		2,000	1,600
On capital stock issue			
At prevailing rate (.25)		2,500	
At year-end rate (.20)		2,000	(500)
On dividend remittance			
At year-end rate (.20)		1,000	
At remittance rate (.22)		1,100	100
On net financial assets			
At beginning rate (.25)		(3,750)	
At year-end rate (.20)		(3,000)	750
On beginning inventory			
At beginning rate (.27)		8,100	
At ending rate (.22)		6,600	(1,500)
On inventory increase			
At year-end rate (.20)		1,000	
At historical rate (.22)		1,100	100
On fixed asset increase			
At year-end rate (.20)		2,000	
At prevailing rate (.21)		2,100	100
On depreciation charges			
At historical rate (.30)		1,500	
At year-end rate (.20)		1,000	(500)
Net income			550

[a]Average rate.
[b]Historical rate.
Source: Compiled by the author.

EXHIBIT 6.5

Illustrative Funds Statement with Exchange Gain and Loss Analysis

	In Local Currency	Funds Flow		Exchange Gain (Loss) in Dollars
		As Shown on Statements	Translated at Closing Rate	
Income from operations	10,000	400	2,000	1,600
Depreciation	5,000	1,500	1,000	(500)
Funds flow from operations	15,000	1,900	3,000	1,100
Proceeds of stock issue	10,000	2,500	2,000	(500)
Total receipts	25,000	4,400	5,000	600
Beginning balances				
Net financial assets	(15,000)	(3,750)	(3,000)	750
Inventories	30,000	8,100	6,000	(2,100)
Total available	40,000	8,750	8,000	(750)
Capital expenditures	10,000	(2,100)	(2,000)	100
Dividends	(5,000)	(1,100)	(1,000)	100
Inventories	(35,000)	(7,700)	(7,000)	700
Net exchange gain or loss		(150)		150
Net financial assets, December 31	(10,000)	(2,000)	(2,000)	0

Statement of Exchange Exposure in Local Currency

	January 1	December 31
Cash	10,000	10,000
Receivables	20,000	25,000
Current liabilities	(25,000)	(25,000)
Long-term loan	(20,000)	(20,000)
Minimum exposure—net financial assets	(15,000)	(10,000)
Inventories	30,000	35,000
Maximum exposure	15,000	25,000

The statement follows the usual format for the funds statement. First, the funds flow from operations is shown. This is followed by additional inflow items. The total receipts are added to the beginning balances to arrive at the total funds available. Since inventories are translated at historical rates, the inventories are shown separately. If they were translated at the closing rate, as are financial assets, this would not be necessary.

The disposition of the funds is shown in the bottom part of the statement. Again inventories must be shown separately since they are not financial assets. The difference between the funds available and the funds outflow represents the ending net financial assets. By deducting the net exchange gain or loss from the historically translated amounts, the amount of the exchange gain or loss is verified.

The net financial assets in local currency can be verified by a separate statement. The accompanying statement of exchange exposure in local currency is designed to show this verification as well as present a management report on the exchange risk in that currency.

EXCHANGE RISK CONTROL

The management report of exchange exposure and risk analysis is used for working capital decisions. The decision process assumes the establishment of cash flow centers. The movement through the cash flow centers is directed by the responsible central financial counsel. With the knowledge of the amounts of exchange risk and exposure, measures can be taken to respond to projected exchange rate fluctuations.

Means of Offsetting Risk in Foreign Exchange

The direction of the exchange risk control measures will depend on the trend of the exchange rate movements. A tendency for devaluation will require a different, an opposite, reaction from a measure to avoid an exchange loss on an upward revaluation. The following measures might be used to protect against imminent devaluation of a currency:

1. Minimize the foreign cash balance by transferring excess cash to the parent company through payment of provisional dividends, paying accounts payable due in other currencies as rapidly as possible, purchasing goods for resale or use, investing excess cash in hard currencies, reducing the parent company investment.

2. Maximize conversion of foreign currency receivables into cash by reducing credit terms, offering generous cash discounts, discounting the receivables.

3. Optimize the inventory risk by accumulating inventories of types on which prices can be raised, maintaining low levels of inventories with inelastic price structures, invoicing export sales in harder currencies.

4. Maximize use of local short-term liabilities by obtaining local borrowing to offset local monetary asset exposure, gaining more generous terms for trade payables, delaying tax payments where possible.

5. Use other hedging devices such as forward exchange contracts, swap arrangements.

Where a currency has a tendency toward an upward revaluation, the exchange loss can be minimized or exchange gain maximized by utilizing the same measures but in the exact opposite direction.

IMPLEMENTING THE WORKING CAPITAL CONTROL PROGRAM

Effective control of the foreign exchange risk will not be assured unless there are formalized information systems directed at its control. Interviews with accounting executives of several multinational industrial corporations bear out the fact that a threefold approach is essential to a successful working capital program. The three requirements for implementation are a formally established policy and reporting procedure, local participation, and a central financial counsel.

A Formal Policy and Reporting Procedure

The best formal policy is a written one. It should include delineation of administrative responsibility, methods of hedging, exposure control techniques, and instructions and formats for the reporting procedures. The procedures should include statement formats for exchange exposure, present coverage, and the details of intercompany accounts. The reporting should be promptly at month's end.

Local Participation

The reports should be translated into the parent company currency before submission by the subsidiary officials. If there is one key to the failure or success of such a program, it is the translation requirement. When the local managers see the translated reports initially, they can be of most help in the administration of the program.

Another important but less critical local duty is the reconciliation of the intercompany accounts with other subsidiaries. Copies of intercompany account recapitulations should be forwarded to affected subsidiaries and reconciled by the subsidiaries before final submission.

Central Financial Counsel

Finally, the whole program must be administered by a central financial counsel. The counsel can be an individual or a committee, and can be located in the headquarters or in a regional office. Nevertheless, the central individual or committee must be versed not only in the overseas units' foreign exchange requirements but also in foreign exchange market trends. International banking institutions may be looked upon to provide advisory assistance; nevertheless, the determination and authority for actual currency conversion must come from the central financial counsel.

In conclusion, it must be noted that the program for managing foreign exchange risk should be an open-ended decision model. It should be a skeleton model, but comprehensive. It should be simple, yet adaptive to many situations.

NOTES

1. National Association of Accountants, *Management Accounting Problems in Foreign Operations,* N.A.A. Research Report 36 (New York: NAA, 1960), p. 66.
2. Ibid., pp. 22-23.
3. William R. Furlong, "How to Eliminate the 'Plugging' of Net Worth for Translated Foreign Currency Financial Statements," *Management Accounting* 49, no. 8 (April 1968): 39-45.

7

FOREIGN INVESTMENT DECISION MAKING

Accountants in international corporations are giving more and more attention to control of foreign exchange risks, projection of exchange risks in foreign investment decision making, and risk evaluation methods in continuing international operations. Each of these segments of the international management accounting process is important. Particularly important is the efficient integration of the investment decision making into the multinational firm's control program.

The integration of investment decision making into the enterprise control program is accomplished by using the established foreign exchange risk, which is designed to integrate the financial control and management accounting reporting system. The financial statement model is used to budget the amount at risk. This allows an analysis and evaluation of the projected risk.

BUDGETING THE AMOUNT AT RISK

Measuring the Amount at Risk

The first management step in the information system involves the measurement of the amount at risk. This is a financial reporting and budgeting problem. Local currency budgets must be prepared to project the future amount at risk. Four pro forma statements—the balance sheet, the statement of owners' equity, the earnings statement, and the statement of financial assets flow— should be prepared.

First, the amount of capital investment in plant and equipment must be determined in the capital expenditure budget. The amounts of the capital expenditures are then integrated into pro forma balance sheets and income statements for the life of the investment. The income statements show not only the depreciation charges but also the funds flow from internal operations. External equity capital sources are shown on the separate pro forma statements of owners' equity.

Then, the source and disposition of funds must be determined in budgeting the foreign exchange exposure. Various relationships and trends must be assumed in projecting the amount at risk; Exhibit 7.1 provides an example. The underlying assumptions in preparing the illustrated local currency pro forma financial statements are:

1. An initial investment of $6,000 (LC 6,000) is made through equipment import and foreign exchange transfer.
2. Local financing is available for the initial financial assets.
3. The plant investment has a five-year lifespan with no salvage value; straight-line depreciation is used.
4. Dividends are paid in local currency at the year-end for the amount of local currency earnings.
5. Local currency net profit margin of 20 percent is maintained before depreciation charges.
6. The foreign country has a 10 percent annual rate of inflation. Costs rise with the inflation; selling prices are increased as costs rise.
7. Production and inventories are stable during the five-year span, and output is readily sold at the established prices.
8. Repatriation of capital is available at the end of the fifth year.

Each assumption must be carefully weighted in the final determination of local currency budgets.

Projecting the Risk Itself

The next information system requirement is the measurement of the risk itself. The real risk has two parameters—the estimated size of future devaluations or revaluations and the projected timing of these occurrences. Economic and political considerations are the determinants. The key economic factor is the inflation rate, particularly in relation to the parent company's economy. Besides internal political factors, external factors such as changes in the rules of the international monetary system must be weighted. Nevertheless, the risk must be projected in order to provide the exchange rates to be used for translation of budgeted statements in the local currency.

EXHIBIT 7.1

Budgeted Local Currency Financial Statements

	Year					
	0	1	2	3	4	5
Balance Sheets						
Financial assets	1,000	1,900	2,790	3,669	4,536	–
Inventory	1,000	1,100	1,210	1,331	1,464	–
Plant assets (net)	5,000	4,000	3,000	2,000	1,000	–
Total assets, December 31	7,000	7,000	7,000	7,000	7,000	–
Financial liabilities	1,000	1,000	1,000	1,000	1,000	–
Equity capital	6,000	6,000	6,000	6,000	6,000	–
Retained earnings	–	–	–	–	–	–
Total equities, December 31	7,000	7,000	7,000	7,000	7,000	–
Statements of Owners' Equity						
Balance, January 1	–	6,000	6,000	6,000	6,000	6,000
Capital contribution	6,000	–	–	–	–	(6,000)
Add earnings	–	1,000	1,200	1,420	1,662	1,928
Less dividends	–	(1,000)	(1,200)	(1,420)	(1,662)	(1,928)
Balance, December 31	6,000	6,000	6,000	6,000	6,000	–
Earnings Statements						
Sales	–	10,000	11,000	12,100	13,310	14,641
Less cost of sales						
Beginning inventory	–	1,000	1,100	1,210	1,331	1,464
Costs and expenses	1,000	8,100	8,910	9,801	10,781	10,249
Less ending inventory	(1,000)	(1,100)	(1,210)	(1,331)	(1,464)	–
Net cost of sales	–	8,000	8,800	9,680	10,648	11,713
Funds flow from operations	–	2,000	2,200	2,420	2,662	2,928
Less depreciation	–	(1,000)	(1,000)	(1,000)	(1,000)	(1,000)
Net income	–	1,000	1,200	1,420	1,662	1,928
Statements of Financial Assets Flow						
Funds flow from operations	–	2,000	2,200	2,420	2,662	2,928
Add beginning inventory	–	1,000	1,100	1,210	1,331	1,464
Less ending inventory	(1,000)	(1,100)	(1,210)	(1,331)	(1,464)	–
Financial assets flow from operations	(1,000)	1,900	2,090	2,299	2,529	4,392
Add capital investments	6,000	–	–	–	–	(6,000)
Less capital expenditures	(5,000)	–	–	–	–	–
Dividends	–	(1,000)	(1,200)	(1,420)	(1,662)	(1,928)
Increase in financial assets	–	900	890	879	867	(3,536)
Financial assets, January 1	–	–	900	1,790	2,669	3,536
Financial assets, December 31	–	900	1,790	2,669	3,536	–

Source: Compiled by the author.

The translated statements will expose the amounts of foreign exchange gains and losses. Exhibit 7.2 shows the translation of the Exhibit 7.1 statements, assuming an exchange rate which is constantly decreasing at an annual rate of 10 percent. With fluctuating exchange rates, exchange gains and losses will derive in the translation process. The amounts of these gains and losses appear as separate items on the translated dollar income statements and the statements of financial assets flow.

Note that, unless remedies are sought, the exchange losses are continually increasing. Common remedies for reducing the foreign exchange risk losses are local borrowing, use of forward exchange contracts, prompt remittance of excess cash, and use of cash to purchase goods for resale or use. Also, the selling price may be increased to compensate for higher costs; but, it should not normally be raised to absorb foreign exchange losses, too. Such a pricing policy, contributing to the inflationary trend, would be self-defeating. If possible, the exchange losses should be hedged or budgeted in the normal operations management. Thus, the budgeting of the future risk is the key to a successful foreign exchange risk control program.

THE ANALYSIS AND EVALUATION OF THE PROJECTED RISK

The next step in the information system is the evaluation of the risk in conjunction with the financial control and budgeting function. The minimum exchange exposure is most often defined as equal to net financial assets. Maximum exposure includes the inventories. Ideally, the maximum exposure should be zero. To avoid losses on devaluation, zero exposure must exist at all times, not only at the reporting date. This means that any inflow must be as carefully managed as are the amounts on hand.

The control is accomplished through a proper analysis of the potential losses. An effective analytical means is to use a funds flow approach as illustrated in Exhibit 7.3. First, the annual funds statements are translated at rates expected to prevail at the time of the transactions. Then, the statements are again translated but at the expected year-end closing rates. The differences derived from this dual translation show the sources of exchange gains and losses. They show the importance of budgeting both the source and use of funds. The decisive elements for the evaluation of the project, then, are the cost of placing capital, the availability and cost of financing, and the availability and cost of foreign currency remittances.

Cost of Placing Capital

Capital placement in a foreign country can be accomplished through foreign exchange transfer, investment in kind, reinvestment of earnings, and

EXHIBIT 7.2

Budgeted Translated Dollar Financial Statements

		Year				
	0	1	2	3	4	5
Balance Sheets						
Financial assets	1,000	1,727	2,306	2,756	3,098	–
Inventory	1,000	1,000	1,000	1,000	1,000	–
Plant assets (net)	5,000	4,000	3,000	2,000	1,000	–
Total assets, December 31	7,000	6,727	6,306	5,756	5,098	–
Financial liabilities	1,000	909	827	751	683	–
Equity capital	6,000	6,000	6,000	6,000	6,000	–
Retained earnings	–	(182)	(521)	(995)	(1,585)	–
Total equities, December 31	7,000	6,727	6,306	5,756	5,098	–
Statements of Owners' Equity						
Balance, January 1	–	6,000	5,818	5,479	5,005	4,415
Capital contribution	6,000	–	–	–	–	(3,726)
Add earnings	–	727	653	593	545	508
Less dividends	–	(909)	(992)	(1,067)	(1,135)	(1,197)
Balance, December 31	6,000	5,818	5,479	5,005	4,415	–
Earnings Statements						
Sales	–	9,524	9,524	9.524	9,524	9,524
Less cost of sales						
Beginning inventory	–	1,000	1,000	1,000	1,000	1,000
Costs and expenses	1,000	7,714	7,714	7,714	7,714	6,668
Less ending inventory	(1,000)	(1,000)	(1,000)	(1,000)	(1,000)	–
Net cost of sales	–	7,714	7,714	7,714	7,714	7,668
Funds flow from operations	–	1,810	1,810	1,810	1,810	1,856
Less depreciation	–	(1,000)	(1,000)	(1,000)	(1,000)	(1,000)
Less exchange losses	–	(83)	(157)	(217)	(265)	(348)
Net income	–	727	653	593	545	508

(continued)

(Exhibit 7.2 continued)

			Year			
	0	1	2	3	4	5
Statement of Financial Assets Flow						
Funds flow from operations	–	1,810	1,810	1,810	1,810	1,856
Add beginning inventory	–	1,000	1,000	1,000	1,000	1,000
Less ending inventory	(1,000)	(1,000)	(1,000)	(1,000)	(1,000)	–
Financial assets flow from operations	(1,000)	1,810	1,810	1,810	1,810	2,856
Add capital investments	6,000	–	–	–	–	(3,726)
Less capital expenditures	(5,000)	–	–	–	–	–
Dividends	–	(909)	(992)	(1,067)	(1,135)	(1,197)
Increase in net financial assets	–	901	818	743	675	(2,067)
Add financial assets, January 1	–	–	818	1,479	2,005	2,415
Less exchange losses	–	(83)	(157)	(217)	(265)	(348)
Financial assets, December 1	–	818	1,479	2,005	2,415	–

Source: Compiled by the author.

loans or other nonequity financing. The cost of the investment is determined by the exchange rate at which the foreign capital investment is transacted. This cost must be compared with the long-run return on investment. The return on investment is measured by the ultimate repatriation of that investment plus the dollar withdrawals of earnings. The investor assumes the risk of exchange rate fluctuation from the time of investment until the time of earnings withdrawal or capital repatriation.

If an investment is accomplished by supplying equipment or machinery, the exchange rate existing at the time of investment is generally considered to be the determinant of the investment cost. Also, when earnings are reinvested, the capital cost is calculated at the exchange rate prevailing at the time of earnings realization. Again, this cost must be compared with the ultimate rate of return that is expected to be derived from the added investment.

Cost and Availability of Financing

A relatively cheap method of investment may be local currency borrowing, particularly if the loans are used to minimize the amount of net financial assets at risk. Sometimes, such loans may be obtained at preferential or guaranteed rates, which are registered with the appropriate local governmental agency or the central bank. The exchange rate may be higher than the free market rate; also, the interest rate on such loans may be higher than interest rates available in other countries. But, in the face of possible devaluations, the added cost may be offset by potential savings in foreign exchange losses.

Another method of financing is the swap transaction arranged between the parent corporation and its foreign subsidiary. There are many other external sources of borrowing, including the Eurobond market, the World Bank group, and development banks. A list of internal and external sources is presented in Exhibit 7.4. Loans appear to be the most widespread source of funds in the international scene. When loans or swap arrangements are utilized, the interest cost must be measured against the projected savings on foreign exchange devaluations.

Finally, equity capital sources may be utilized. The availability of local equity financing will depend on the sophistication of the foreign capital market, the availability of local private capital, and the opportunities in joint ventures. The cost of equity capital must be weighted against the advantages of local participation.

The Cost and Availability of Foreign Currency Remittances

In some countries local financing may not be obtainable. Where this is the case, the cost of the capital investment is directly related to the cost and availability of foreign currency remittances.

The foremost thought before investment is the feasibility of the earnings withdrawals. Coupled with the availability of the withdrawals is the exchange rate at which the remittances can be transacted. The next consideration is the availability and cost of the eventual repatriation.

The lack of availability of remittances causes blocked earnings. If such blocked amounts cannot be invested locally at favorable rates of return, currency devaluations will cause a continuing erosion of the investment. A way to avoid blocked foreign exchange is to obtain foreign currency remittances through exports, simply by having the foreign subsidiary imports billed in the parent company's currency. However, such procedures are often prohibited or at least regulated by a country's trade laws.

Finally, availability of remittances will depend on the earnings potential and working capital position of the foreign enterprise.

THE FINAL DECISION PROCESS

After the available resources and projected return are determined, the investment decision model can be adjusted accordingly. If more than one alternative appears feasible, additional management accounting techniques should be used. First, the projected flows of funds initially and as repatriated

EXHIBIT 7.3

Analysis of Foreign Exchange Losses on a Budgeted Investment Venture

	In Local Currency	Financial Assets Flow — In Dollars		Exchange Gain (Loss) in Dollars
		As Shown on Statements	Translated at Closing Rate	
Year 1				
Funds flow from operations	2,000	1,810	1,818	8
Add beginning inventory	1,000	1,000	909	(91)
Less ending inventory	(1,100)	(1,000)	(1,000)	—
Financial assets flow	1,900	1,810	1,727	(83)
Less dividends	(1,000)	(909)	(909)	—
Exchange loss	—	(83)		83
Financial assets, December 31	900	818	818	—
Year 2				
Funds flow from operations	2,200	1,810	1,818	8
Add beginning inventory	1,100	1,000	909	(91)
Less ending inventory	(1,210)	(1,000)	(1,000)	—
Financial assets flow	2,090	1,810	1,727	(83)
Less dividends	(1,200)	(992)	(992)	—
Exchange loss	—	(157)		157
Financial assets, January 1	900	818	744	(74)
Financial assets, December 31	1,790	1,479	1,479	—

Year 3

Funds flow from operations	2,420	1,818	8
Add beginning inventory	1,210	909	(91)
Less ending inventory	(1,331)	(1,000)	–
Financial assets flow	2,299	1,727	(83)
Less dividends	(1,420)	(1,067)	–
Exchange loss	–	–	217
Financial assets, January 1	1,790	1,345	(134)
Financial assets, December 31	2,669	2,005	–

Year 4

Funds flow from operations	2,662	1,818	8
Add beginning inventory	1,331	909	(91)
Less ending inventory	(1,464)	(1,000)	–
Financial assets flow	2,529	1,727	(83)
Less dividends	(1,662)	(1,135)	–
Exchange loss	–	–	265
Financial assets, January 1	2,669	1,823	(182)
Financial assets, December 31	3,536	2,415	–

Year 5

Funds flow from operations	2,928	1,818	(38)
Add beginning inventory	1,464	909	(91)
Financial assets flow	4,392	2,727	(129)
Less capital repatriation	(6,000)	(3,726)	–
Dividends	(1,928)	(1,197)	–
Exchange losses	–	(348)	348
Financial assets, January 1	3,536	2,196	(219)
Financial assets, December 31	–	–	–

Source: Compiled by the author.

EXHIBIT 7.4

Sources of Financing

External

Letters of credit
Commercial bank loans
    Parent country bank
    Local country bank
    Third country bank
    Branch of an international bank
    International bank group or consortium
Credit through government institutions
    Export-Import Bank
    Agency for International Development
    Overseas Private Investment Corporation
    Foreign Credit Insurance Association
Eurodollar or Asian-dollar financing
    Commercial bank intermediary
    Foreign finance subsidiary
    Eurobond (and Euroequities) market
Financing through World Bank group
    International Bank for Reconstruction and Development
    International Development Corporation
    International Finance Corporation
Credit through development banks
    Regional development banks such as the Inter-American Development
      Bank
    National development banks
    Private development banks such as the Atlantic Development Group for
      Latin America
Equity Financing
    Parent company
    Subsidiary
    Joint ventures

Internal

Generated from operations (retained earnings before deduction for depreciation
    and depletion)
Extended from the parent, through informal cash advances, formal loans, or
    supplied inventory
Extended from another subsidiary or an affiliate by advancing cash or supplying
    inventory

Source: Compiled by the author.

could be adjusted to present values, with discounting at a normal rate of return. Furthermore, probabilities could be established for each of the alternatives. The final solution may be an optional multiple approach to financing.

The use of the financial statement model for budgeting the amount of risk allows a view of the outcome based on certain assumptions. By formalizing this model, perhaps through a computer routine, the assumptions can be changed slightly for testing the sensitivity of the outcomes to minor changes in the assumed facts. Further, the model can be used to establish a flexible budgeting system whereby changes in the environmental factors can be analyzed. Finally, once the final investment decision is made with its assumed environmental criteria, the established budget can be utilized for comparison with actual data as the data are accumulated over time. The investment decision-making model then serves also as a control device.

8

THE MULTINATIONAL
INTERCORPORATE
TRANSFER SYSTEM

For many multinational companies the transfer of goods and services among overseas units is an almost daily occurrence. The primary type of transfer is the movement of manufactured goods. However, there also can be transfers of raw materials acquired in a single country as well as royalties, service fees, and home office allocations.

Two management issues evolve in the transfer process. First, there must be a determination of the amount of the transfer as dictated by the transfer price or fee. Then, there must be the settlement of the transaction.

TRANSFER POLICY

The Principle of Equity

The principle of equity has emerged as the underlying philosophy in establishing a formal transfer policy.[1] Under this principle, the multinational firm sets its transfer policy on the basis of a reasonable and equitable allocation of the profits among the overseas units, as can be justified by a long-run host country interest in development and investment growth in the foreign country.

The principle of equity may seem to be contrary to a goal of total corporate profit maximization. Yet, short-run sacrifices may be feasible when the eventual effects of a fair, equitable transfer policy optimize the long-run profit goal and firm survival.

Policy Considerations

Uniformity in policy administration appears to cease once the goal of equitable distribution is established. Because of the many factors to be considered in an equitable allocation, most company transfer policies remain somewhat flexible. For example, the income tax factor may cause variations in policy administration among subsidiaries. However, just as important are such factors as export subsidies and tax incentives, customs duties, exchange rate risk, expropriation risk, inflation risk, exchange controls, the level of competition, and the financial appearance of the subsidiary.

When the transfer policy conflicts with the performance evaluation system, dual records may be necessary to reflect the effects of the transfer policy as compared to the effects under an accurate profit center concept. The profit center concept also may be somewhat adjusted to link profit with an effort such as the maintenance of quality. Also, further record keeping may be necessary in some countries in order to comply with federal and local regulations.

The Transfer Price

When the policy considerations are coupled with the principle of equity, the use of "arm's length" prices emerges as the most prevalent practice.[2] Their use allows a flexibility in favorably weighing a particular country's considerations in an equitable fashion. This may cause variations in application among countries. Nevertheless, "arm's length" prices are the most widely used because a policy based on such prices can be the most easily justified.

Negotiated prices and prices based on cost-plus are further methods used to apply the transfer price policy. Negotiated prices are arranged between the buying and selling units. Negotiation may be particularly necessary when the product is not sold to outside parties. The price can be based on cost-plus which includes an allocation of home office overhead to cover the marketing, distribution, and promotion expenses.

From a firmwide profit maximization viewpoint, use of below-cost pricing based on relevant incremental variable costs may be considered profitable in some cases, particularly when such pricing leads to additional sales to provide incremental profits through use of duplicated idle facilities. However, such a pricing policy may be criticized as a low-price dumping of products in the importing country.

On the other hand, prices may be purposefully inflated to cover costs of royalties and other service fees which cannot be taken as a deductible business expense in some countries. Also, the inflated price method may be utilized to offset the blocking of dividend remittances.

Whether prices are equitable, or sometimes inflated or depressed, is a policy determination. What is important to note, however, is that the price determines the amount of the fund transfers among countries as well as the profit allocation. The settlement of the transfers has a direct effect on a country's balance of payments.

TRANSFER SETTLEMENT

The multinational corporation's intercompany account settlements may involve payments of foreign currencies among a dozen or more overseas units. There may be many unnecessary currency conversions, particularly if each foreign subsidiary receives payment for its intercompany receivables and makes payment for its intercompany payables. The quantity and amount of such conversions should be optimized. To do so requies a settlement policy that is clear and consistent. A clear policy puts the transfer settlements on a routine basis, while a consistent policy makes the settlements less vulnerable to losses from exchange rate fluctuations. An optimal settlement policy also requires the establishment of reporting procedure as well as a decision process.

The Reporting Procedure

The multinational company may already have a regular monthly financial reporting system for its subsidiaries. Information on the intercompany account balances should be an integral part of the subsidiary reporting system.

At the subsidiary level the month-end intercompany balances are first reconciled by each subsidiary. If any intercompany accounts between subsidiaries do not agree, the subsidiaries' controllers are made responsible for reconciling the difference and determining the proper amounts. In this manner, any in-transit items are neither omitted nor double-reported in the overall reconciliation of the amounts. After the relevant information has been transmitted to the appropriate subsidiary units, the adjusted reports are forwarded to headquarters.

The Netting Process and Its Advantages

The subsidiary reports are then recapitulated at headquarters in order to determine the net balances; here, companies may use the netting process. An example of the process as applied to intercompany settlements is presented in

Exhibit 8.1. The reconciliation in Exhibit 8.1 shows the intercompany balances in foreign currency and the amounts translated into the parent company currency. It shows each subsidiary's payables and receivables. The offset is either the total payable or total receivable, whichever is lower. After deducting the offset, the net balance receivable or payable results.

The amounts of the offsets between each subsidiary's receivables and payables are communicated to each subsidiary, for only the net balances need to be transferred to accomplish complete settlement of the intercompany balances. In the illustration, only two subsidiaries, A and C, must forward payments; the other subsidiary, B, and the parent company are to receive the amounts. Note that the net balances amount to only one-third of the total payables.

The netting process may reduce the number of currency conversions but always reduces the amounts of the transfers. For example, if the next month-end recapitulation is the same as presented in Exhibit 8.1, except that the amount owed by B to A is $2,000 more, then the offset of A increases to $15,000 and B's offset increases to $14,000. The net result then is that only the parent company is to receive its $16,000 payment, the amount to be sent from subsidiary A ($1,000) and subsidiary C ($15,000). Thus, the number of conversions is reduced to only two, and the amounts of the transfers are reduced by more than 70 percent.

The Cost-Benefit Decision

The netting report provides the information for the international money management decision process. The responsibility for the decision making is preferably centralized at the headquarters.

The netting process may effect direct cost savings—for example, by reducing conversion costs through mere transfers in an international bank.[3] Further savings may be achieved by internal hedging—that is, by withholding intercompany transfers to increase exchange exposure positions in countries with a high probability of predicting an expected currency revaluation. However, such savings must be measured against the benefits of an efficient movement of working capital and the costs of borrowing if a subsidiary's working capital position becomes inadequate. Nevertheless, without a deliberate settlement policy and procedure, such cost-benefit factors may be neglected in the intercompany transfer settlement decisions.

Direction and Control

Once a decision is made, however, the central authority directs the payments to be processed. Instructions are advanced to the units as to the

EXHIBIT 8.1

Recapitulation of Intercompany Account Net Balances of a U.S. Corporation with Foreign Subsidiaries in France, Germany, and Italy

Receivable by	Parent's Payables	Payables of Foreign Subsidiaries A	B	C	Total Receivable	Payables Offset	Net Receivables
Parent corporation		$10,000	$8,000	$2,000	$20,000	$4,000	$16,000
Subsidiary A (5.12 francs = $1)	FR5,120 $1,000		FR10,240 $2,000	FR51,000 $10,000	$13,000	$13,000	0
Subsidiary B (3.22 deutsche marks = $1)	DM6,440 $2,000	DM9,660 $3,000		DM28,980 $9,000	$14,000	$12,000	$2,000
Subsidiary C (582 lira = $1)	L582,000 $1,000	L1,746,000 $3,000	L1,164,000 $2,000		$6,000	$6,000	0
Total payables	$4,000	$16,000	$12,000	$21,000	$53,000	$35,000	
Receivables offset	$4,000	$13,000	$12,000	$6,000			
Net payables	—	$3,000	—	$15,000			$18,000

Source: Compiled by the author.

amounts to be transferred. The instructions may not necessarily require complete monthly settlements if internal hedging is practiced. For example, prior to the floating of the deutsche mark, the German subsidiary (B) in the above illustration may have been required to withhold its intercompany payables even though its receivables were settled.

Thus, the conversions are directed in light of the exchange exposure position of each country and the related currency risk predictions. Feedback on the performance of the instructions then becomes the final step in the reporting procedure. It is accomplished by merely reviewing the intercompany positions as communicated in the subsequent monthly reports.

THE NEED FOR CENTRALIZED CONTROL

Foreign exchange is one of the greatest risk factors in multinational financial management. Product and service transfers to, from, and among foreign subsidiaries complicate the control of this risk. The intercompany transfers thus require a cybernetic system that not only informs on the quantity and amounts of the transfers but also directs the movement of the settlements. Such a system is best controlled by a central financial authority.

The flow of intercompany transactions has a direct contributory influence on the short-run performance of the foreign operating unit. The performance is affected not only by the movement of intercompany transfers but also by the settlement of the transfer transaction and by the price that determines the amount of the fund movement. The centralized authority can best evaluate the inflationary, exchange market, cost structure, and fund movement factors within an integrated control system.

The Control System

With a dependence on the modern instant data-moving communicative methods, the budget becomes the main core in centralized control. The budget is used in control by comparing its projections with the actual results as time passes. The total budget procedure includes the capital budget as well as an operational budget as depicted in Exhibit 8.2. The budget system breakdown is necessary to separate the working capital and operations control functions from the investment decision-making and capital control functions. Each subsidiary may be given autonomy within the operational budget.

The budget must be in consonance with the international strategic plan. The strategic plan that involves investment decision making requires problem-solution techniques and should present projections for several years hence. In

EXHIBIT 8.2

The Movement of Funds

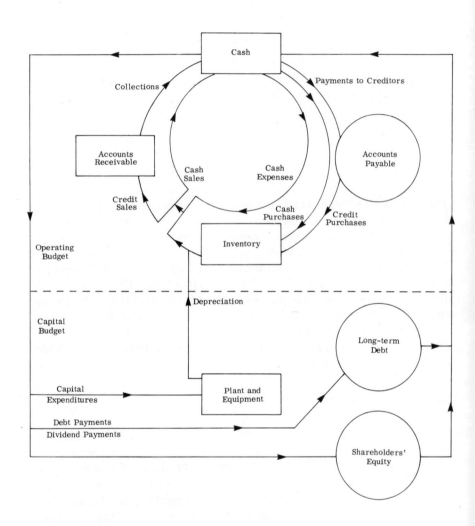

Source: Compiled by the author.

EXHIBIT 8.3

The Movement of Intercompany Transfers

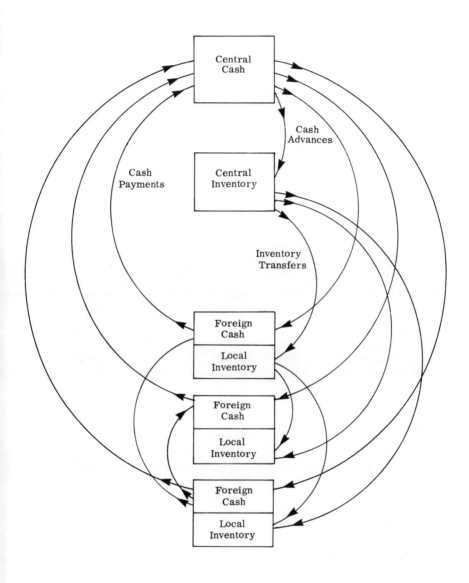

Source: Compiled by the author.

the general plan, as well as in routine decision making, social responsibility should be included as a qualitative factor. The determination of the social consequences of possible alternatives may need to be accomplished intangibly. Instances of the social responsibility awareness include the local employment considerations, which help the community, as well as the national and international nature of the firm's output, which benefit society in general.

The strategic plan is a general future plan with specific projections for the capital budget. Operations control, in contrast, is quite concrete and is centered on the financial reporting system as a key to the system of operational budget performance. Operational control is primarily a responsibility of the foreign management with the coordination integration of the reporting system as part of the duties of the international controller.

The Control Centrum

Though operational control may be centered on the overseas profit center, international coordination is accomplished through the centralized control center in the headquarters. The centralized control is necessary to enhance an expedient movement of goods and services among the affiliates. The flow of goods and services initiates the movement of funds (see Exhibit 8.3). International reporting and instructional dissemination of the movement of funds is integrated into the centralized information system.

Centralized control may not be popular for a multinational corporation, but it may be necessary to assure minimization of currency conversion costs and foreign exchange losses. With the current flux in the international monetary scene, the centralized control of the currency conversions may indeed be an important financial management responsibility.

NOTES

1. James Greene and Michael G. Duerr, *Intercompany Transactions in the Multinational Firm* (New York: National Industrial Conference Board, 1970), pp. iv-vi.
2. Ibid., pp. 21-23.
3. "Are Currency Exchange Costs Nibbling at Your Overseas Profits? " *Business Abroad* 95, no. 2 (February 1970): 14-15.

IV

COMPARATIVE INTERNATIONAL
ACCOUNTING PRINCIPLES

9

GENERALLY ACCEPTED
WORLDWIDE ACCOUNTING
PRINCIPLES

Current trends in the accounting field point toward a worldwide uniformity of accounting principles, particularly for corporations with wide stockholder distribution. The trends toward uniformity are stimulated by a desire for comparability in the worldwide investment community. If an advanced stage of uniformity is to develop, an understanding of the differences among nations is necessary. This chapter highlights some of the most relevant differences.

Uniformity expedites the training of accounting apprentices, increases the reliability of national statistics, and aids in federal and local tax administration. Uniformity also tends toward a rational development of accounting theory.

Flexibility, the opposite of uniformity, supposedly permits better adaptability of accounting methods in each firm, each industry, or each type of transaction. Furthermore, as long as a single method is not dictated, experimentation is allowed. New and better theories may result. The theories may even allow the adaptation of the accounting recording policies in a managerial control system. Nevertheless the pressure toward uniformity is overwhelming.

UNDERLYING CONCEPTS

Basic Assumptions

On the international level, the going-concern, consistency, and accrual concepts are accepted as fundamental accounting assumptions.[1] The going-

concern and accrual concepts are utilized on a worldwide basis. The two
concepts imply the use of the matching principle—matching cost and revenue as
related to the period reported on the income statement. Also implied is the use
of the revenue realization principle, which dictates that revenue not be
recognized until cash is received or unless the right to receive cash is coupled
with definite assurance of collection.

The consistency assumption also has received a worldwide acceptance.
That accounting principles be applied on a consistent basis has not been
expressly required, however, in some countries such as Switzerland and Italy.
Furthermore, many countries do not require the disclosure of the effect of a
change in accounting principles when a principle has not been consistently
applied.

Other Conventions

Three important governing considerations also have been accepted at the
international level.[2] These are the concepts of prudence, substance over form,
and materiality.

The prudence concept is related to the principle of conservatism in the
United States. It assumes a proper use of judgment when uncertainties require
some choice in applying a principle. The intuitive but conservative use of proper
judgment is widely accepted as necessary in all parts of the world. Just as widely
accepted is the related concept of substance over form, which indicates that
transactions are accounted for in accordance with economic reality rather than
with their legal form.

The materiality concept assumes the proper disclosure of all relevant
financial statement items—also widely accepted around the world. One major
exception is the lack of disclosure for hypothecated or pledged assets. Further,
the lack of disclosure of departures from the consistency concept in some
countries assumes a similar lack of adoption of the materiality concept with its
basic inherent disclosure requirement.

The Historical Cost Concept

Probably the most basic concept in traditional accounting is the historical
cost concept. It is accepted worldwide. However, departures from cost, such as
appraised values or market values, also are quite often used. Unfortunately,
departures from cost are not always disclosed in the financial statements. The
lack of disclosure is most often coupled with the fact that the departures are in
accordance with tax provisions requiring that tax accounting and accounting for
financial reporting purposes be synchronized. The most quoted example of such
a case is the West German reporting requirement. Another good example is the
financial and tax reporting requirement in Colombia.

Inflation in many countries has caused criticism of historical cost-based financial statements. However, alternative price-level adjusted statements or current-value statements have not been adopted to replace the use of historical cost. The alternatives are being promoted as supplementary statements, at least at the present time. There is one well-known exception: in Brazil, companies may have to adjust the balance sheet carrying values by a coefficient as determined by a federal authoritative body.

ASSET PRINCIPLES

Receivables

One of the first principles promulgated by the U.S. accounting profession at the time that the Securities Act was passed in 1933 was the requirement that receivables from officers and directors be shown separately on the balance sheet. Though the reporting standards of many countries now also require such separate disclosure, a considerable number of countries do not have strict reporting requirements for receivables from officers and directors. Strangely enough, more countries had adopted standards that force the separate reporting of receivables from affiliated companies.

In determining the amount of receivables, the worldwide accounting practice is to report the receivables at net realizable value. It assumes the adoption of the allowance method of writing off uncollectible accounts based on a rounded-off average of expected uncollectibles as determined by past experience and future projections. In a few countries, such as Italy, Spain, and the Philippines, tax laws do not allow a deduction for uncollectible accounts until an account is definitely ascertained to be uncollectible. Where such tax laws exist, the adoption of the direct-write-off method for recording uncollectible accounts expense may be expected to be quite prevalent.

Inventories

The rule of valuating inventories at cost or market, whichever is lower, has worldwide acceptance. However, there are differences as to the definitions of cost and market and as to the method of assigning costs.

The term market can have variant meanings not only in different countries but also according to types of inventories. For work in progress and finished goods, net realizable value is most often used. Net realizable is also widely used for resale merchandise. Replacement cost is not widely used for resale merchandise but is more often applied to raw materials inventories. In only a few countries a deduction for normal profit is made to determine the amount of net realizable value. Also, in a few countries, a write-down to realizable value can be reversed in a later period if the realizable value increases.

In cost determination, the weighted-average and FIFO methods of assigning costs to inventories are the most generally acceptable in all parts of the world. The last-in-first-out LIFO and base-stock methods are allowed and used in a few countries. Also widely acceptable is the retail method for determining costs of resale merchandise. For manufactured goods inventories, and work in progress, cost includes all direct materials and direct labor plus all variable and fixed factory overhead costs based on a normal capacity. However, utilization only of direct costs or of prime costs is acceptable in some countries. In this connection, direct costs include variable factory overhead costs whereas prime costs include only direct labor and direct materials.

Departures from the cost-or-market rule are rare but nevertheless do exist. The departures vary from upward adjustments for inflation to downward adjustments for the purposes of inventory reserves established by the authority of tax laws. The most outstanding example of reporting inventories above cost is the utilization of replacement cost accounting in the Netherlands. By contrast, in Sweden and in Switzerland, inventories may be written down to below either cost or net realizable value to establish a valuation reserve which actually understates the inventory valuation on the balance sheet.

With the wide variation in acceptable inventory reporting standards, disclosure of accounting policies is necessary in international financial reporting. The disclosure of the basis of carrying inventory and of types of inventories is widely practiced. Unfortunately, the method of cost determination has not always been disclosed. Particularly unfortunate is the acceptable practice in some countries not to disclose undervalued inventories which create secret reserves. Perhaps the establishment by the IASC, in 1975, of the international accounting standard for reporting inventories and stating inventory accounting policies will enhance the proper disclosure of inventories.[3]

Investments

The rule of cost or market, whichever is lower, is also acceptable on a worldwide basis for reporting of investments. It is applied to marketable securities held on a short-term basis and to long-term investments. This means that an impairment in value of a long-term investment requires a write-down to reflect the net realizable value. Its application is extended to investments reported on an equity basis. On an equity basis, the carrying value of an investment includes the original cost plus the investor's share of undistributed earnings since acquisition.

The equity method of accounting for long-term investments originated in the United States, has been adopted in Canada and Mexico, and is spreading to other parts of the world. The equity method is spreading as a consolidation concept, requiring its use for investments in affiliates that are effectively controlled through partial ownership—for example, by ownership of between 20 and 50 percent of the voting shareholder interest. As a consolidation concept, the equity method is applied in consolidated financial statements which are used to combine a parent company's financial statements with those of subsidiaries that are over 50 percent controlled. Its application would apply as well to unconsolidated subsidiaries and joint ventures, though in many countries such investments are reported at cost. However, in most countries, the financial statements do disclose the market value if the reported amount varies significantly from the market value.

Compared to its use as a consolidation concept, the equity method as an accrual concept has not been as widely adopted. As an accrual concept, the method would require recording by the parent company. Thus, when parent company statements are prepared without consolidation, the retained earnings and reported earnings would be the same as if the financial statements were consolidated. It may be expected that the third international accounting standard, established by the IASC in 1976, will give impetus to a uniformity in the use of the equity method of accounting as well as in the consistency in the practice of preparing consolidated financial statements.[4]

Property, Plant, and Equipment

The generally accepted amount for reporting property, plant, and equipment is at cost less accumulated depreciation. In a few countries, certain assets such as land may be recorded at fair economic value. As noted above, one method used in Brazil is to annually adjust the asset carrying value according to a federally determined price-level coefficient. On the other hand, a depreciable asset may be written down if the book value exceeds the fair economic value. However, in many countries, the cost-less-accumulated depreciation principle is so totally adopted that even fully depreciated assets are kept intact in the accounts.

The generally accepted rule for reporting fixed assets assumes a full disclosure of the amount of accumulated depreciation. Furthermore, there is a worldwide practice of segregating assets among main categories, showing assets such as land as a separate balance sheet item. And, whether in footnotes or on a funds statement, there is usually a disclosure of capital expenditures that are currently made as well as those that have been firmly contracted.

Intangibles

A general worldwide practice is to record only purchased intangible assets and to amortize the cost over the estimated useful life. However, goodwill recorded in the acquisition of a subsidiary is handled in a diverse manner around the world. Amortization varies from none at all to a direct charge to the acquiring company's retained earnings. When it is accomplished, the amortization is often over an arbitrary period, say five years, in accordance with specific corporation laws.

There is also a variation in the determination of acquired goodwill and for handling negative goodwill. In some countries, particularly the United States and Mexico, the difference in cost and the book value of acquired net assets is first assigned to assets and liabilities where identifiable. Any remaining difference is termed goodwill. Negative goodwill in the United States, Canada, Mexico, and a few other countries is first used to reduce noncurrent assets. In the United States and Canada, the remainder is amortized to net income. In contrast, a few countries do not permit the recording of negative goodwill nor the amortization to income but require that such amount be credited directly to the shareholders' equity. Needless to say, the controversy over the treatment of goodwill that has existed in the United States is evidently prevailing among other nations.

EQUITY PRINCIPLES

Liabilities

The widespread practice is to present the amounts of both definitely determinable and estimated liabilities on the balance sheet. Also, the amounts of payables to affiliates and to officers and directors, and the existence of contingent liabilities, are disclosed in most countries. The disclosure is not elaborate, or omitted, in some countries—for example, in Spain and Italy. Further, in only a few countries, the amount of self-insurance beyond the normal risk is disclosed.

Generally, the payment terms including interest rates are disclosed for long-term liabilities. However, there is an important variation in the method for handling of bond discount and issue costs. Three different methods are used around the world: the bonds-outstanding method whereby the bond discount and issue costs are amortized over the life of the debt in relation to the amounts outstanding; the straight-line method whereby the costs are amortized over the life of the debt in equal amounts each year even if the amount of bonds outstanding declines; and the direct write-off method whereby the costs are written off at the time of issuance. Though the balance sheet distortions caused by the variation may not be significant, the effects in analyzing a corporation's interest expense may be misleading.

Invested Capital

In the countries where stock options, stock warrants, and preferred stocks are issued, disclosure is usually made as to the respective preferences and the potential effect on the number of outstanding shares. The reacquisition of issued shares—that is, the acquisition of treasury stock—is prohibited in the open market in many countries. However, there is a wide range of treatments when corporations do disclose the amounts of legally acquired treasury stock. Showing treasury stock as an asset, as a deduction from stockholders' equity at cost, or as if the shares were retired are methods practiced in different countries.

Another accounting practice that varies among countries is the treatment of stock dividends. The method of charging the retained earnings for the amount of market value, as is the practice in the United States, is used in only a few countries. More prevalent is the practice of charging retained earnings for the amount of the par or legal value of the shares.

Equity Reserves

Many types of equity reserves are utilized around the world: revaluation reserves, legal reserves, appropriated retained earnings reserves, and general reserves. Since the various reserves serve different purposes, an understanding of each is necessary for an investor analysis of owners' equity.

Though revaluation reserves are used rather scatteredly in a number of countries, their use is most prevalent in the Netherlands where replacement cost accounting has been modeled. In the Netherlands, where the revaluation reserves are established to write up depreciable assets to replacement cost, the depreciation charges on the incremental write-up are not recorded through the income but are charged directly to the revaluation reserves. The reason for this procedure is that the incremental depreciation expense is not deductible for income tax purposes. The alternate procedure is to charge the incremental depreciation as an allocated expense, with a parallel entry transferring an equivalent amount from the revaluation reserve to retained earnings. In many countries, the transfer to retained earnings may be considered to be superfluous since the revaluation reserve can be charged for stock dividends. In a few countries, even cash dividends can be declared from revaluation reserves.

Legal or statutory reserves are required in many countries. The legal provisions for the reserves vary somewhat among countries. Generally, an annual percentage, for example, 10 percent, of income must be credited to the legal reserve with a maximum provision, say 20 percent, of total paid-in or legal capital. Since dividends cannot normally be charged against a legal reserve, the amount acts as an additional protection to creditors.

Appropriated retained earnings reserves are voluntary reserves which can later be transferred back to the unappropriated retained earnings account. Normally, such reserves are not used to absorb charges to income. The amounts so established merely act as a temporary restriction of retained earnings. The use of this reserve is not very widespread.

Quite widespread in usage is the general reserve which, in some respects, is similar to the appropriated retained earnings reserves. However, in some countries, notably Switzerland, the reserve can be utilized to smooth income among periods. Generally, the movement in reserve accounts is fully disclosed in the financial statements.

Retained Earnings and Dividends

In many countries, any restriction of retained earnings is disclosed. An excellent example of such a restriction is an amount of cumulative preferred dividends in arrears. Furthermore, in a number of countries, provisions must be established for dividends proposed for ratification at the subsequent annual meeting.

In the United States and Mexico, where the pooling-of-interest method is used in the accounting for mergers, the retained earnings of the merged company are accumulated retroactively. Since the pooling method is not a generally accepted international principle, an awareness of its effects may be important for an investor's analysis.

INCOME STATEMENT PRINCIPLES

Revenues

The generally accepted accrual concept assumes a proper cutoff in regard to sales. In most cases, the exchange in a sale transaction is assumed to take place at the time of delivery. Exceptions are made in most countries when the collection on credit transactions is not reasonably assured. In real estate transactions, for example, unrealized gains are generally deferred until collection is assured. Accruing profits on the basis of percentage of completion for long-term contracts is also generally accepted.

One revenue recognition rule that is applied in the United States is not generally applicable: the financing method of accounting for lease revenue. In the United States, when the ordinary risks and rewards of a lessor are transferred to the lessee, the transaction is recorded as an installment sale rather than as an operating lease. The substance of such transactions take precedence over the legal formality.

Depreciation

The concept of depreciation is generally defined to mean a rational and systematic allocation of the cost of buildings, equipment, and other depreciable assets. The most widely used allocation method is the straight-line method. The accelerated depreciation methods such as the sum-of-the-years'-digits method and the percentage-of-declining-balance method also have some acceptance. Used little are the unit-of-production method, the composite-rate method, and the sinking-fund method. All these methods are assumed to be applied when the method is considered to best allocate the original cost in a systematic and rational manner.

There are some exceptions to the general concept of depreciation. For example, in Switzerland, an ultraconservative attitude in regard to depreciation may cause an excess depreciation charge in the early years of an asset's life. On the other hand, in a number of South American countries, the depreciation expense is exaggerated by the adjustment of the asset cost with a centrally determined index. Thus, the depreciation policies, depreciation charges, depreciation rates, and accumulated depreciation amounts, and the original costs as well as the written-up value increments, should all be disclosed. Such disclosure is often presented in footnotes as well as in financial statements. Because of the significance of the amount of the depreciation charge for most firms, the disclosure requirement should be mandatory.

Income Taxes

In the United States, the amount of the income tax expense is shown on the income statement. The amount is recorded on an accrual basis. The U.S. practice is found prevalent in most countries. The main exception in the handling of income tax charges is in tax allocation accounting.

Some countries require that accounting records be maintained in accordance with tax regulations. In those countries, tax allocation is inappropriate. Where tax regulations do not require a synchronization of tax records with accounting records, tax allocation may become necessary. For example, in Canada and the United States, tax allocation is required to account for timing differences, between the time the tax is accrued and the time it is paid. Comprehensive tax allocation is utilized, and the deferred taxes are not adjusted for future tax rate changes. This method of allocation is called the deferred technique, which is in contrast to the liability method. The liability method, which is allowed in the United Kingdom, dictates an adjustment of the amount of deferred tax to reflect current tax rates. In other countries, no deferred taxes at all are established but are merely mentioned in footnotes. Furthermore, the division of such deferred taxes between the current portion and the long-term portion is required in the United States but is not always disclosed in other countries.

Other Expenses

Since the accrual concept has worldwide adoption, the differences in the recording of expenses should not be significant. However, the following differences in expense recognition are noteworthy.

In Switzerland, the accrual concept is not followed dogmatically; for example, costs of sales may not be matched with sales. In Italy, bonuses to corporate directors are recorded as direct charges to retained earnings. In

Germany, a commendable practice is to charge all unrealized exchange gains and losses and exchange adjustments on unsettled balances to income in the period of the exchange rate change. In the United States, Canada, Italy, and Japan, the estimated pension costs must be accrued over the term of employment rather than "paying-as-you-go," a practice followed in many countries. Also, the U.S. practice of accruing losses on purchase commitments is not universally followed. The only present solution to these variations is to require disclosure so that proper analysis can be achieved.

Earnings Per Share

Finally, an important statistic used by sophisticated security analysts is the earnings-per-share computation. The presentation of this statistic on the income statement is beginning to gather momentum. It is presented on financial statements prepared in the United States, Canada, the United Kingdom, the Netherlands, the Philippines, and a few other countries. Most of these countries show a fully diluted earnings per share when complex capital structures exist. However, the simple, most important earnings-per-share figure is computed differently among the leading countries. A primary earnings-per-share computation is based on an average of common shares outstanding plus common share equivalents, as practiced in the United States, Mexico, and the Philippines. In Canada and the United Kingdom, a fundamental earnings-per-share computation is based only on common shares outstanding. Needless to say, when variations exist in the computation of the security analysts' most basic data, an understanding of comparative international accounting principles inevitably becomes desirable.

The purpose of this chapter was to highlight some of the worldwide accounting variations. The differences can be exaggerated. Certainly, there are many similarities in the adoption and utilization of accounting policies around the world. Yet when differences exist, comparability of financial statements is hindered. Pressure from the investment community can be expected. The trend toward uniformity is increasing.

NOTES

1. International Accounting Standards Committee, *Disclosure of Accounting Policies,* International Accounting Standard no. 1 (London: IASC, 1974). See also the following primary sources for this chapter: American Institute of Certified Public Accountants, *Professional Accounting in 30 Countries* (New York: AICPA, 1975); Haskins and Sells, *International Tax and Business Services—Reporting, Accounting, and Business Practices Abroad* (New York: Haskins and Sells, 1972); and Price Waterhouse International, *Accounting Principles and Reporting Practices—A Survey in 38 Countries* (Toronto: Price Waterhouse International, 1973).

2. International Accounting Standards Committee, op. cit., p. 4.

3. International Accounting Standards Committee, *Valuation and Presentation of Inventories in the Context of the Historical Cost System,* International Accounting Standard no. 2 (London: IASC, 1975).

4. International Accounting Standards Committee, *Consolidated Financial Statements and the Equity Method of Accounting for Investments,* International Accounting Standard no. 3 (London: IASC, 1976).

10

SOCIAL ACCOUNTING
CONCEPTS

A new pattern of development appears to be emerging, concerned with expanding the accounting dimension to include social responsibility stewardship. The development broadens the user audience for traditional financial statements and expands the accounting process to new types of social reporting. A review of some of these emerging social accounting concepts is relevant to the study of comparative international accounting principles.

The social accounting concepts can be placed in three main categories. First, there is the social responsibility reporting for the firm. This represents an extension of the financial statement audience to those readers who have an interest in the social effects of the policies of the public-owned enterprise. Secondly, there is developmental accounting, which is concerned with the promotion of economic development and the reporting of the effects and stages of such development. Finally, there are the macroaccounting concepts, which expand the accounting dimension to the neglected areas of national income accounting and of national and global planning.

SOCIAL RESPONSIBILITY ACCOUNTING

The expansion of social responsibility has impelled the accountant to consider reporting the effects of certain social costs, expenditures, and benefits. Welfare accountability is coupled with environmental accountability as a new dimension for accountants; political accountability represents a further addition for the accounting profession. Thus we have the birth and development of socioeconomic accounting.

Socioeconomic accounting reports on the performance of social programs and social institutions. Social institutions employ a system of fund accounting. Social programs can be integrated with the fund accounting system of a not-for-profit entity or within a governmental unit. The types of funds are: current unrestricted, restricted, endowment, loan, annuity, plant, and agency. The stress on the fund arrangement and its data accumulation is designed to report on the stewardship accountability for expenditures funded. Audit guides have been published to deal with the financial reporting problems.[1] However, socioeconomic accounting should extend beyond a mere reporting of expenditures.

Socioeconomic accounting also should be designed to measure the social benefits, or costs, involved with social programs. A set of socioeconomic principles must be established. Such a set of precepts can be expressed as follows:[2]

1. Clearly set forth standards for measurement when making fund appropriations for those objectives for which the social program or agency exists.
2. Keep changing the mix of resource inputs—that is, the kind of things being sought with the budgeted funds—until satisfactory results are achieved.
3. Use the existing qualitative measurement standards in the social, education, and welfare areas—standards which are now being overlooked in assessing these nonbusiness operations.
4. Establish a marketplace mechanism, or at least create feedback reporting procedures among the clients of the social programs.
5. Use discretionary fund allocations as an executive incentive device.
6. Merge two or more agencies which are too small to be effective.
7. Divest deficient units of an otherwise effective agency.
8. Regularly prepare social reports for qualitative accomplishments, as well as the usual financial reports.
9. Fix responsibility for applying socioeconomic accounting principles.
10. Establish a regular program of socioeconomic audits by independent outsiders.

Social programs are administered directly by social not-for-profit enterprises and governmental entities. The programs are not restricted to social institutions but are also fulfilled through business enterprises. The programs may be directly administered through contributions to social organizations or indirectly by expenditures that benefit society. One method of socioeconomic reporting is to prepare a socioeconomic operating statement, tabulating separately the expenditures made voluntarily for improving the welfare of employees, the public safety of the company's product or services, and the conditions of the environment.³ A socioeconomic operating statement may be particularly applicable to multinational enterprises which participate in the social progress of foreign countries. The statement may be designed to fulfill the requirements of a code of conduct for multinational enterprises. Political contributions could also be reported in the socioeconomic operating statement.

Political Accounting

Related to social responsibility accounting, political accounting is concerned with accounting for the politician and for political contributions.

Accounting for the politician is centered on the principles for preparation of personal financial statements. In the United States, the accounting profession has sanctioned the use of current values in personal financial statements. Current values tend to provide more relevant data for the voting citizen than do historical costs, particularly when the disparity is considerable. The promulgated report is a two-column financial statement showing both the cost basis and the current-value basis.⁴ The purpose is to give the citizen a relevant financial presentation so as to allow a judgment about a politician's possible conflict of interests and the inherent personal integrity capabilities.

The other element of political accounting is the stewardship accounting for political contributions. More and more attention is being given to suggesting the publication of a financial statement of the total campaign contributions and expenditures by each political candidate. Further, public-owned corporations are being asked to report political contributions and favors, if given, in the financial statements to shareholders.

ACCOUNTING IN DEVELOPMENT

Accounting in development has been receiving attention due to its reflection of the worldwide social responsibilities of idealistic citizens. The efforts toward a code of conduct for multinational enterprises shows the significance that is being placed in assistance to development. Accounting information plays an important role in determining and monitoring the financing requirements and economic effects in the various stages of development of firms and their operations within an economy.

Three stages may be identified in the development process of an economy. Prior to the first stage of development, the economy assumedly has many small firms with limited operational capacities. The firms are probably using a type of cash basis accounting with a major emphasis on the flow of immediate return to the owner-managers. The first stage of development may be named the take-off stage, with the introduction of new products and/or capacity expansion.

After the takeoff stage, the economy enters a drive-to-maturity stage in the development process. Finally, the economy enters the mature stage of high mass production and consumption.[5] Firms may enter stages of development that parallel the development of an economy. Firms can, however, also enter similar stages of development regardless of the stage of economic development.

Accounting in Development-Stage Enterprises

Particular attention to accounting in development-stage enterprises is now being given in the United States;[6] the problem involves the expending of start-up costs. The start-up efforts include financial planning; raising capital; exploring for natural resources; developing natural resources; establishing sources of supply; acquiring property, plant, and equipment; recruiting and training personnel; developing markets; and starting up production. When these costs are immediately charged to income in the period incurred, a retained earnings deficit will accumulate before net profits commence. Full disclosure of the nature of such enterprises must be given in the financial statements.

The principles for development-stage enterprises assume a successful operational performance in due time. Costs are deferred only if they are recoverable and matchable with specific future benefits. The going-concern assumption prevails. Thus, specific disclosures are required in order to identify the development-stage reasons for a temporarily reflected poor performance.

Accounting During Development

As firms develop within themselves and in relation to a developing economy, the accounting requirements exert a broadening responsibility for the management accountant and the professional public accountant. The primary functions of accounting in developing countries should be financial reporting to various individuals and groups external to the firm, financial reporting to management, and business advising to management.[7]

As the economy grows and firms grow in size and development, additional sources of financing usually are sought. The main sources of financing may be financial institutions. Another source of financing may be issuances of bonds or stocks to the public. In any case, external reporting becomes more and more important as a firm develops, particularly within a developing economy. As the complexity of the firm grows, the need for extensive internal management reporting also becomes essential. Management reporting focuses on internal control, cost control, pricing decision making, and working capital management. Internal management reports may also provide data for investment decisions through use of such techniques as break-even analysis, sensitivity analysis, market analysis, and personnel performance evaluation. Finally, business advisory services may be extended to management by accountants in developing companies. This service may include tax counseling, but also management advisory services regarding management control and financial management. The services may be performed by the firm's controller and treasurer or by the outside professional accountant.

During development, the functions of the accountant broaden to take in the more complex responsibilities and the more sophisticated counsel. Education becomes essential in assuring that the practicing accountant has the professional competence to perform the developmental duties. Thus, emphasis on education and training is very important in accounting in development. Another important aspect of accounting in development is the overall need for accounting information in administering developmental programs.

Economic Evaluation Accounting

Economic evaluation accounting assumes an accounting structure that is designed to provide information which facilitates the economic evaluation of an enterprise's activities by management, investors, and government.[8] It provides information for analysis of the firm's activities in relation to the economic goals of a nation. It requires that accounting for the effects of certain economic incentives be in accord with the objectives of the incentives.

Economic incentives for development may be in the form of subsidies, tax credits, or regulatory control. The incentives may be rather direct and for a special purpose such as an investment tax credit or a dividends exclusion provision. Or, the incentives may be rather general such as a subsidy for location in a certain underdeveloped area. What is important is that the reporting be so designed as to allow ready analysis of the results and effects of the incentive utilization. The implications are that the accounting for economic evaluation must enhance the control of economic incentives and the achievement of economically designed goals. Idealistically, the economic evaluation accounting objective should be linked with a macroaccounting system.

MACROACCOUNTING

Macroaccounting is an area of accounting that extends the traditional entity stewardship to total governmental reporting. Typically, accounting for governmental units such as townships, school districts, and government-owned enterprises has been treated as an element of microaccounting—that is, as accounting for a firm. At least the entity concept of a firm is postulated to apply to such governmental entities though other accounting concepts such as going concern and accrual are not utilized in pure form in accounting for all such entities. Since this book is concerned with identifying emerging trends, the tempting discussion of where microaccounting stops and macroaccounting commences is dispensed with here. There will merely be a view of the nature of governmental accounting and national income accounting.

Governmental Accounting in a Free Market System

Governmental accounting, commonly called fund accounting, is designed to facilitate control over expenditures of a particular governmental unit. The units include counties, townships, municipalities, school districts, and special districts such as port authorities, libraries, and public buildings.[9] Accounting for such units is segregated into the following types of funds: general, special revenue, debt service, capital project, enterprise, trust and agency, intragovernmental service, and special assessment.[10] The principles for governmental accounting are quite well developed in the United States. Some universities offer separate courses on the subject.

Absent from the groups of entities covered in the typical governmental fund accounting discussions are national governments. However, attention is being given to this matter too; a proposal for presentation of consolidated financial statements for the U.S. government has been formulated (see Appendix). With additional effort and counsel form the accounting profession, governmental financial reporting may be expected in the future to be more responsible and receptive to the social interests of the taxpaying public.

Governmental Accounting in a Controlled Economy

In a controlled economy, the governmental enterprise includes not only the governmental administration but all the industrial, financial, transportation, and utility enterprises of the nation. A sample list of balance sheet account classifications for a controlled economy is presented in Exhibit 10.1. The unique items are the distributive assets and special purpose sources. The accounts listed could be used to draw up a balance sheet that would be similar to the statement of financial position for a governmental enterprise fund.

If the enterprises' financial statements in the controlled economy were all consolidated, many of the accounts would be eliminated in consolidation. The intercompany accounts, including accounts with other enterprises and with the central administration, consist of distributive assets, monetary assets except for the cash on hand, receivables, credits, obligations, and internal source accounts. The resulting consolidated balance sheet would present a total of all the assets in the country. The preparation of an equivalent statement of financial position for a noncontrolled economy goes beyond national income accounting.

EXHIBIT 10.1

Account Classifications in the Soviet System

Assets

Productive Assets
  Fixed assets
    Buildings, machinery and equipment, installations
    Accumulated depreciation (contraaccount)
    Capital repair
  Production stocks
    Raw materials and supplies
    Inexpensive and fast-depreciating objects
    Accumulated depreciation on inexpensive and fast-depreciating objects
      (contraaccount)
    Spare parts for current repairs
  Costs of production
    Basic production
    Shop costs
    General factory costs
    Costs of future periods
Circulating assets
  Finished production
    Finished articles
    Outside productive expenses
    Production shipped to buyers
  Monetary assets
    Cash
    Account at central bank
    Special account for financing long-term investments
  Accounts receivable
    Purchasers and customers
    Personal accounts
Distributive assets
  Diverted assets
    Payments to be made to the budget
    Payments to be made to banks on long-term investments
    Deductions into special funds

Sources

Internal sources
  Basic activity
    Invested capital
    Reserve for future payments
    Profits and losses
  Special purpose
    Amortization fund for capital repair
    Special funds
    Special financing
External sources
  Credits
    Short-term loans from central bank
    Long-term credits of banks
  Suppliers
  Obligations
    Accounts with the budget
    Workers and employees
    Deductions for social insurance
    Amortization fund subject to payment to bank for long-term investment

---

*Source:*Bertrand Horwitz, *Accounting Controls and Soviet Economic Reforms of 1966* (Evanston, Ill.: American Accounting Association, 1970), pp. 11, 13.

National Income Accounting

National income accounting, sometimes referred to as macroaccounting, is concerned with movements of funds in the business, households, and government sectors of the economy; in domestic savings and investment; and in the rest of the world. It is also concerned with the computation of the gross national product which includes wages, rental income of persons, net interest paid to households, profits, indirect business taxes, business transfer payments, and capital consumption. The system determines national income which is the gross national product less capital consumption and indirect business taxes. The preparation of a statement of financial position has been excluded.

National income accounting has traditionally been an endeavor associated with economists. Only now is the accounting profession giving it much attention. The precedent-establishing inclusion of the topic in an advanced accounting textbook will hopefully reinforce the trend toward inclusion of macroaccounting concepts as part of the basic knowledge of the accountant.[11] Further extension of the concepts will predictably set forth a system for preparation of balance sheets for the whole economy and eventually for the whole world.

Global Accounting

At the present time, international accounting at the governmental and national level is limited to balance-of-payments accounting. Balance-of-payments accounting reports the movements in trade and finance among countries. Each nation is particularly interested in achieving a favorable balance of trade whereby merchandise and service exports exceed merchandise and service imports.

By nature, not all countries can have favorable trade movements at the same time. As macroaccounting concepts are extended beyond national income accounting to financial position and funds flow reporting, the frontier will be opened to simulation of national macroaccounting reports in a global system. Perhaps the balance-of-payments analysis can then be more receptive to the social goals of a worldwide society.

NOTES

1. For example, American Institute of Certified Public Accountants, *Audits of Voluntary Health and Welfare Organizations* (New York: AICPA, 1974); AICPA, *Audits of Colleges and Universities* (New York: AICPA, 1973); and AICPA, *Hospital Audit Guide* (New York: AICPA, 1972).

2. David F. Linowes, "The Accounting Profession and Social Progress," *Journal of Accountancy* 136, no. 1 (July 1973): 34.

3. David F. Linowes, *The Corporate Conscience* (New York: Hawthorn Books, 1974), pp. 104-37.

4. American Institute of Certified Public Accountants, *Audits of Personal Financial Statements* (New York: AICPA, 1968), pp. 2-3.

5. Surendra S. Singhvi, *Corporate Financial Management in a Developing Economy* (Seattle: University of Washington, Graduate School of Business Administration, 1972), pp. 48-49.

6. Financial Accounting Standards Board, *Accounting and Reporting by Development Stage Enterprises,* Statement of Financial Accounting Standards, no. 7 (Stamford: FASB, 1975).

7. George M. Scott, *Accounting and Developing Nations* (Seattle: University of Washington, Graduate School of Business Administration, 1970), p. 75.

8. Ibid., pp. 149-66.

9. American Institute of Certified Public Accountants, *Audits of State and Local Governmental Units* (New York: AICPA, 1974), p. 4.

10. National Committee on Governmental Accounting, *Governmental Accounting, Auditing and Financial Reporting* (Chicago: Municipal Finance Officers Association, 1968), p. 3.

11. See Charles H. Griffin, Thomas H. Williams, and Kermit D. Larson, *Advanced Accounting* (Homewood, Ill.: Richard D. Irwin, 1971), pp. 722-71.

PART

V

**INTERNATIONAL FINANCIAL
REPORTING TO INVESTORS**

11

FINANCIAL STATEMENT
PRESENTATION PRINCIPLES

The public corporation operating in the international environment must provide meaningful financial statements for the international investor. In doing so, the financial executive is faced with the selection of a proper reporting currency. When there are international operations, an appropriate approach to the translation of the foreign currency transactions and foreign currency financial statements must be considered. Consistent with this translation process, the financial executive must decide upon a proper perspective for consolidation of foreign currency financial statements.

THE REPORTING CURRENCY

The enterprise operating in the international environment must have a reporting currency which most clearly reflects the transactions of the enterprise. It is necessary to use one currency so that the total entity provides financial information based upon a common denominator. This is necessary both for the management of the enterprise and for proper interpretation by the international investor.

Generally, there are considered to be several approaches to the selection of a reporting currency. There are: the legalistic approach, using the currency of the country of incorporation; the business transactional approach, using the currency in which the majority of the business transactions are negotiated; the ownership approach, using the currency of the country where the majority of stockholders are domiciled; the dividend approach, using the currency in which the dividends are paid; the strong currency approach, using the currency that has worldwide recognition as a strong currency; and the central unit currency approach, using an established or imaginary currency unit which may be in terms of a monetary unit of a precious metal content or involve the mix of several strong currencies.[1]

The Legalistic Approach

The most normal situation is when a corporation uses the currency of the country in which it is incorporated. The laws of some countries, such as Germany, indeed require that firms incorporated in that country have their financial statements prepared in the currency of that country. However, the home currency is not always used. For example, there are a number of foreign companies listed on the New York and American stock exchanges which use U.S. dollars as their reporting base because the majority of their business transactions are in U.S. dollars.

The Business Transaction Approach

Basing the reporting currency selection on the majority of the monetary transactions in which the enterprise operates has a strong practical support. It eliminates the need to hedge a large quantity of foreign risk exposure in a country in which it holds its majority of assets.

The Ownership Basis

The citizenship of the shareholders may be considered in the determination of the proper recording currency. Ownership would seem to be a popular basis for the choice of currency. After all, the annual report is prepared for the owner—that is, the stockholder. But serious shortcomings beset the use of ownership as a basis for choosing a currency. For one thing, ownership interests may change, and for another, a multinational corporation may have shareholders domiciled in many countries. Moreover, the firm may not necessarily invest and operate in any particular country at a continuous or stable rate. Thus, the ownership basis is not a good criteria for selecting the currency of account.

The Dividend Approach

The dividend approach could also be used as an alternative for choosing the currency base. Financial statements prepared under this concept would preferably be stated in the currency in which the dividends are paid. As a matter of fact, however, corporations do issue dividends in a currency other than the one used as the reporting currency. For example, in 1970 three Canadian corporations listed on the New York and American stock exchanges paid dividends in Canadian dollars but used the U.S. dollar as the reporting currency. On the other hand, two other Canadian corporations paid U.S. dollar dividends but continued to express their financial statements in Canadian currency.[2] One can thus conclude that the dividend considerations are not the key element in the reporting currency decision.

The Central Currency Unit Approach

A currency unit such as the special drawing rights of the International Monetary Fund or the basket currencies used in the Euromarket or in Central America could be used as a generally accepted worldwide currency. For example, the European Currency Unit (ECU), the official European unit of account (EUA 17), and the unofficial European unit of account (EUA 9) are used in the transactions of governments in the European Economic Community. Also, the European composite unit (EURCO) is used for private contracts. The Eurco is an established mix of currencies, as shown in Exhibit 13.1, with specific values and proportional weightings changing on a day-to-day basis in line with fluctuation in the foreign exchange markets.[3] The advantage of the use of such a reporting currency is that the financial statements would tend to have a more stable common denominator, particularly if the majority of business is transacted in the several currencies constituting the currency mix.

Perhaps some day such an accepted worldwide common currency unit can be used for financial reporting. In the meantime, the use of the currency in which the majority of business transactions takes place would appear to be the most theoretically sound. For international corporations operating from a center in one country, the transaction basis would coincide with the legal basis representing the currency of the country of incorporation. In any case, the reader of the international financial statements should not be misled in the analysis of the statements. The country of incorporation and the currency base should clearly be stated on the face of the financial statements.

THE TRANSLATION METHOD

Once the financial executive has selected the reporting currency, he must use the appropriate method of translating foreign currency business transactions or foreign currency account balances. If there are international operations managed through a subsidiary or branch, the branch or subsidiary financial statements accumulated in a foreign currency must be translated into the reporting currency. The degree of decentralization of control will play a part in the translation process.

EXHIBIT 11.1

The European Composite Unit of Currency (EURCO)

	0.90	Deutsche Marks
plus	1.20	French Francs
plus	0.075	Pounds Sterling
plus	80.00	Italian Lira
plus	0.35	Dutch Guilders
plus	4.50	Belgian Francs
plus	0.20	Danish Kroner
plus	0.005	Irish Pounds
plus	0.50	Luxembourg Francs
equals	1.00	EURCO

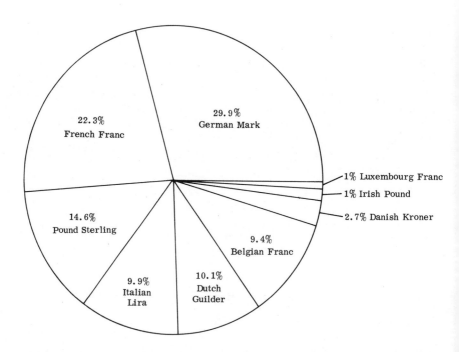

Source: Bryan Williams, "A Common European Currency," *Management in a World Perspective* (Los Angeles: University of Southern California, School of Business, 1975), pp. 30-39.

The Two-Transaction Approach for Translating Foreign Currency Business Transactions and Foreign Currency Account Balances

The two-transaction approach reflects the view that the collection of a receivable or payment of a liability is a transaction separate from the original sale or purchase transaction. The original transaction is translated at the exchange rate in effect on the date of the transaction. Any monetary balances and other balance sheet amounts carried at realizable value must then be adjusted to reflect the current exchange rate in effect on the balance sheet date. Any change in the exchange rate does not affect the amount recorded as export revenue or import cost at the time of the original transaction.

In contrast to the two-transaction approach is the one-transaction approach which dictates that the amount of the import or export transaction not be determined until the final settlement. The method of settlement of an open balance is a decision separate from the original import or export transaction. Accordingly, the decisional effects of exposure to an exchange rate change should be recorded separately as an exchange gain or loss in the period that the exchange rate changes. The two-transaction approach to recording international business transactions is receiving worldwide support in practice.

The Transaction Approach to Translation of Foreign Currency Financial Statements

When a firm expands its export and import business by setting up a branch or subsidiary, it must translate the foreign currency financial statements in order to condense them with the home office statements. In order to preserve the historical cost concept in translation, a transaction approach similar to the two-transaction approach has developed. Through experience, the approach has been refined and has received various names.

The current-noncurrent method of translating foreign currency financial position statements evolved in the early twentieth century in the United States. This method used current exchange rates to translate working capital items and changes. Research studies in the 1950s indicated a departure from the current-noncurrent method that had been formally promulgated in the AICPA's Accounting Research Bulletin no. 4 issued in 1939. Practice showed the tendency toward using a monetary-nonmonetary method. This method, which translated monetary items at current exchange rates, was formally advocated by the issuance of Opinion no. 6 by the Board in 1965. However, the translation problem was subsequently studied in depth, culminating in the publication by the AICPA of Accounting Research Study no. 12 in 1972.[4] This study conceptualized the monetary-nonmonetary method into the theory founded on the temporal principle. The study also recognized another method—the current rate approach—which was strongly supported in other countries.

The Temporal Principle for Translation

With the issuance of Financial Accounting Standard no. 8 by the FASB, the temporal principle was formally adopted in the United States in 1975. The temporal principle is based on a parent company perspective. It assumes that all transactions of subsidiaries and branches are transactions controlled and recorded by the parent company. The translation process is concerned with the times, the temporal events, during which the transactions are recorded. In essence, the approach is an extension of the two-transaction approach for translating international import and export transactions. The historical exchange rate, which is the rate prevailing at the time of each transaction, is used to translate original transactions. However, monetary items and balance items representing current values are updated with each exchange rate change. Thus, exchange gains and losses occur as exchange rate changes take place and are recorded as current income items.

The Current-Rate Approach to Translation

The current-rate approach, a method recognized in other countries, uses the exchange rates prevailing on a balance sheet date to translate all financial statement accounts. The method is based on a local perspective, viewing the foreign-based operations as autonomous business enterprises. The unit of measure is the currency of the foreign country of domicile. The translation process is then merely a mechanism for restating the financial statements in the common reporting currency.

Under the current-rate approach, the exchange adjustment derived in the translation process is viewed as an adjustment to the shareholders' equity. The adjustment derives in the updating of the beginning owners' equity. Dividends paid by the subsidiary to the parent as well as other intercompany international transactions may affect the amount of the translation adjustment. Of importance, however, is that, under this approach, the subsidiary remittances and other intercompany payments are viewed as a sacrifice of the working capital of the subsidiary. The dividend is viewed as a payout of the local currency, to be paid to the parent shareholders.

A variation of this method is to use the transaction approach for translating the income statement accounts. The transaction approach is equivalent to the temporal approach and therefore the exchange gains and losses derived would be justifiably reported as current income statement items. In any case, the extent of any widespread utilization of the current-rate approach may depend upon the perspective. If the local perspective taken by the advocates of this method is found to most nearly represent the proper multinational perspective, then this method may develop into the most appropriate for the truly multinational enterprises.

THE CONSOLIDATION CONCEPTS

The perspectives taken under the two evolving translation methods parallel the two most widely accepted consolidation concepts. The factor that causes different views in consolidation is the treatment of minority interests. The financial statement treatment of minority interests in the consolidation process depends upon the view taken on consolidated statements.

The Parent Company Concept for Consolidation

Under the parent company concept, the consolidated statements are viewed as extensions of the parent company statements, in which the investment account of the parent is replaced by the individual assets and liabilities underlying the parent's investment. The subsidiaries are viewed as equivalent to branches. For partially owned subsidiaries, the minority interest is viewed as an outside group, and reported as a liability in the consolidated financial statements. Further, the minority interest share of the subsidiary income is viewed as an expense to the consolidated entity comprising the parent and its proportionate share of the consolidated subsidiaries.

At the date of acquisition, any difference between the cost of the parent's investment and the parent's interest in the net assets of the subsidiary is attributed entirely to the parent company and does not affect the minority interest in the acquired company. Further, when intercompany transactions are eliminated in consolidation, only the parent's share of an intercompany transaction is eliminated, because the minority share in such transaction is considered to be a transaction with outsiders.

The Entity Concept for Consolidation

Consolidated statements, under the entity concept, are viewed as those of an economic entity with two classes of shareholders' equity—the majority interest and the minority interest. These interests are treated consistently as an entity and thus are both treated as portions of the shareholders' equity. The earnings of the entity then are shared proportionately between the two types of interests. The minority interest is considered not as an outside group, but as part of the total ownership equity.

In the elimination of intercompany transactions, all intercompany profits are eliminated, because only transactions outside the consolidated entity are relevant. Also, any excess of the cost of the parent's investment over the parent's interest in the net assets of the subsidiary is used as a basis for revaluing all the assets of the subsidiary, and the minority interest is also revalued accordingly. Thus, this concept views the consolidated entity with international operations as

EXHIBIT 11.2

A Comparison of Two Consolidation Concepts

Parent Company Concept	Entity Concept
Minority interest is treated as a liability on the balance sheet.	Minority interest is treated as a class of owners' equity.
Minority interest share of net income is treated as an expense to the consolidated group.	Minority interest income is treated as a divisional share of the consolidated income.
Only the parent company proportionate share of unrealized intercompany profits is eliminated.	Total elimination of unrealized intercompany profits is achieved by prorating to minority and majority interests.
Any difference between the parent's investment and the parent's interest in the net assets of a subsidiary is allocated to identifiable assets with any remainder shown separately on the consolidated balance sheet.	The excess of the cost of the parent's investment over the parent's interest in the net assets of the subsidiary is used as a basis for determining the fair value of the entire subsidiary with a proportionate amount allocated to the minority interest.

Source: Compiled by the author.

a single multinational enterprise with autonomous, decentralized activities in various countries with variant classes of ownership interests.

Selection of the Appropriate Concept

A comparison of the two consolidation concepts is shown in Exhibit 11.2. The selection of the appropriate concept will depend on the perspective. In this regard, most international corporations now view their overseas operations as extensions of the parent company. Further, the parent shareholders are considered to be the primary reader of the consolidated statements. Thus, it is not surprising to note that the accounting professions in the United States, the United Kingdom, and Canada prefer the parent company concept.[5]

Consolidation of Foreign Subsidiary Price-Level Adjusted Financial Statements

Another conceptual decision arises when foreign currency price-adjusted financial statements are to be consolidated. Two methods, as illustrated in Exhibit 11.3, may be utilized. One method, the translate-restate approach, would price-adjust the translated foreign currency financial statements using the

EXHIBIT 11.3

Two Methods for Consolidating Foreign Subsidiary Price-Level Adjusted Financial Statements

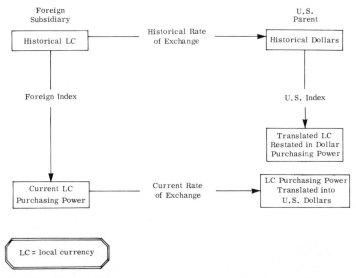

Source: Institute of Chartered Accountants in England and Wales, *Accounting for Inflation* (London: The Curwen Press, 1973), p. 33.

price indices of the country of the parent company, which would assumedly be the reporting currency. Another method, the restate-translate method, would first adjust the foreign subsidiary financial statements using the local price indices of the subsidiary country, and then translate the price-level adjusted statements using the current-rate method of translation.[6]

The approach used depends on whether the parent company perspective or the local perspective is selected for translation. Thus, all the primary concepts of consolidated international financial statements seem to integrate into one major decision as to the proper perspective for the transnational investors.

THE OVERALL PERSPECTIVE

Upon contemplation of the various alternatives involved in the decisions to report consolidated international financial statements, an underlying postulate appears to surface in the various choices: the perspective taken. Strangely enough, there is always a choice between two main perspectives, the parent company and the local. A setting down of the choices in two categories shows some consistency may be necessary in maintaining one perspective. Such a segregation is given in Exhibit 11.4.

Under the parent company perspective, the emphasis is on the parent company and the reporting to its shareholders. This would require use of the

EXHIBIT 11.4

Foreign Subsidiary Consolidation Concepts
under Two Different Perspectives

The Parent Company Perspective	The Multinational Perspective
The reporting currency is the currency of the country of incorporation.	The reporting currency is the currency in which the majority of the business transactions occur.
The temporal approach to translation of foreign currency financial statements is utilized for subsidiaries viewed as extensions of the parent company operations.	The current-rate approach to translation of foreign currency financial statements views the foreign subsidiaries as autonomous operations.
The parent company consolidation concept views the foreign subsidiary operations as extensions of the parent, similar to branches.	The entity concept for consolidation views the consolidated entity as one enterprise with various classes of shareholder interests.
The translate-restate method is utilized for price-adjusting translated foreign currency financial statements.	The restate-translate method is utilized for consolidating translated foreign currency price-adjusted financial statements.

Source: Compiled by the author.

currency of the country of incorporation as the reporting currency. Furthermore, the parent company perspective advocates the use of the temporal approach to translation and the parent company concept for consolidation, with the translate-restate method required for price-level adjustments of translated foreign currency financial statements.

The other alternatives follow another underlying postulate, which is identified as the multinational perspective. This identification is appropriate because the emphasis is on a broader, more international outlook as compared to the parent perspective with its rather centralized home country emphasis. Whether or not each alternative shown in Exhibit 11.4 under this perspective is the preferred may be controversial. Perhaps an integrative approach may be finally resolved as the most appropriate.

In this connection, it would seem appropriate to note that the effects of an adoption of current-value accounting may provide some inertia to an integrative approach. For example, with current-value financial statements, the current exchange rate would be the appropriate rate for translation of foreign currency balance sheets under either the temporal approach or the current-rate approach to translation. Also, the minority interest at date of acquisition would be the same under both the entity concept and parent company concept for consolidation. Indeed, the adoption of current-value accounting on a worldwide basis may lead to international harmony in transnational reporting to investors.

NOTES

1. Gerhard G. Mueller, *International Accounting* (New York: Macmillan Co., 1967), pp. 208-12.

2. Norlin G. Rueschhoff, "U.S. Dollar Based Financial Reporting of Canadian Multinational Corporations," *The International Journal of Accounting* 8, no. 2 (Spring 1973): 108-09.

3. Bryan Williams, "A Common European Currency," *Management in a World Perspective* (Los Angeles: University of Southern California School of Business, 1975), pp. 30-39.

4. Leonard Lorensen, *Reporting Foreign Operations of U.S. Companies in U.S. Dollars,* Accounting Research Study no. 12 (New York: American Institute of Certified Public Accountants, 1972).

5. Accountants International Study Group, *Consolidated Financial Statements* (New York: American Institute of Certified Public Accountants, 1973), par. 73.

6. Paul Rosenfield, "General Price-Level Accounting and Foreign Operations," *The Journal of Accountancy* 131, no. 2 (February 1971): 58-65.

**TRANSNATIONAL FINANCIAL
REPORTING PRACTICES**

Establishing a standard set of international financial statement presentation principles will not, in itself, lead to international harmony in transnational financial reporting to investors. Besides comparability, the international investor may also want an assurance as to the fairness of the presentation. The investor may obtain the assurance through certification by a competent outside auditor. This assumes a high level of universally applied professional standards for auditors.

In this chapter, there is a review of the reporting standards as applied in transnational financial reporting. The review is designed to permit a familiarization as to the present status of professional standards for public accountants. The review is preceded by a study of the form and content of financial statements.

FORM AND CONTENT OF FINANCIAL STATEMENTS

Presentation Principles

In the preceding chapter, presentation principles were outlined for choice of currency, foreign currency translation, and financial statement consolidation. Variations in the principles do exist. Not only are there differences in the choices of principles but also in the methods of applying the principles. Furthermore, there may be inconsistencies in the choice of accounting policies within an overall perspective.[1]

Consolidation policies, for example, are not consistent within the countries around the world. Three specific types of consolidation policies may be identified: consolidated financial statements must be prepared for the parent company stockholders (a U.S. practice); consolidated statements must be prepared as supplementary financial statements to parent company financial statements (a U.K. requirement); and parent company statements need only be presented to the parent company stockholders. The establishment of an international accounting standard for consolidated financial statements should eventually alleviate the problems of consolidation policy differences that allow presentation variations and possible manipulation of profits and losses among a parent company and its subsidiaries and affiliates.

International accounting standards may also be necessary for other presentation policies. For example, the first international accounting standard, established by the IASC in 1974, recommends publication of comparative financial statements presenting the results of the preceding accounting period along with the current year's results. The practice of presenting comparative statements is widespread but not universal. Furthermore, there are some other presentation policy differences that may require more study before transnational financial statement readability can be simplified. Let us examine some of the individual financial statements and their content and format.

The Statement of Financial Position

The most basic financial statement is the balance sheet or statement of financial position. It has been used since the medieval origins of double-entry record keeping. Its use, however, has developed into varied formats. Examples of the typical formats used in four different countries are presented in Exhibit 12.1. The Canadian format is the one used in the United States; it is also used in many other countries including Brazil, Denmark, Japan, and Mexico. An upside-down arrangement of balance sheet categories, such as that shown in the typical German balance sheet, is used in France and the Netherlands. The upside-down arrangement is also used in Australia, although the two sides of the statement are reversed. The most unique arrangement is the one presented for the United Kingdom. Such varied formats do not enhance reader comprehension of the international investors' market.

The variations in format show only the surface differences. Within the segregations, other variations exist. For example, the Brazilian current asset category excludes liquid assets, which are presented separately. In Germany, the long-term liabilities must be due beyond four years; obligations due within four years are shown with other liabilities, which include those most currently due. Also, in Germany as well as in France, the current year's profit is shown separately at the bottom of the balance sheet. If the results of the current year's operations show a loss, the amount is listed at the bottom of the asset side of the balance sheet. A study of how the balance sheet presentation policies evolved

EXHIBIT 12.1

A Comparison of Balance Sheet Formats

Canada

Assets
    Current assets
    Investments
    Fixed assets
    Other assets
Liabilities and shareholders' equity
    Current liabilities
    Long-term debt
    Deferred income taxes
    Shareholders' equity

West Germany

Assets
    Outstanding payments on subscribed share capital
    Fixed assets and investments
    Revolving assets
    Deferred charges and prepaid expenses
    Accumulated net loss (of period)
Liabilities and shareholders' equity
    Share capital
    Open reserves
    Adjustments to assets
    Reserves for estimated liabilities and accrued expenses
    Liabilities, contractually payable beyond four years
    Other liabilities
    Deferred income
    Accumulated net profit (of period)

Australia

Share capital and reserves, and liabilities
    Share capital and reserves
    Long-term debt and deferred income taxes
    Current liabilities

Assets
    Fixed assets
    Investments
    Current assets

United Kingdom

Net assets employed
    Fixed assets
    Subsidiaries
    Associated companies
    Current assets
    Less current liabilities
    Less deferred liabilities
Assets represented by
    Share capital
    Reserves

Source: American Institute of Certified Public Accountants, *Professional Accounting in 30 Countries* (New York: AICPA, 1975), pp. 51, 125-26, 629, 746-49.

may be quite interesting; such a study may be necessary if a consistent, theoretically sound, universally applied presentation principle were to be established.

The Income Statement

A second basic financial statement is the income statement. Its presentations can be very simple and limited, as they are in the United Kingdom, or very elaborate, as in Germany. Examples of statements showing the extremes in presentation are given in Exhibit 12.2.

In Germany, the income statement is based on a production-oriented concept, a principle that is unique to that country. However, in France, a simplified income statement is accompanied by a general operating statement that is also production oriented. The production-oriented income statement does not readily identify the cost of goods sold and is as much concerned with value added as with revenue from sales.

Generally, the basic sales-oriented format used in the United States, Canada, and Japan has been widely adopted. Variations do exist as to the content of the cost of goods sold and the expense breakdowns. Quite often the depreciation charges are excluded from the cost-of-goods-sold section and presented as a separate one-line item. In most countries, the income tax expense is disclosed separately.

EXHIBIT 12.2

A Comparison of Income Statement Formats

United Kingdom

Group turnover
Profit before taxation and extraordinary items
    Less taxation based on profit of the year
Profit after taxation and before extraordinary items
    Extraordinary items
Profits attributable to shareholders of parent company

Japan

Sales
    Less cost of goods sold
Gross profit on sales
    Less selling and general administrative expenses
Operating income
    Add nonoperating revenues
Gross profit for the period
    Less nonoperating expenses
Net income for the period

West Germany

Net sales
Increase or decrease of finished and unfinished products
Other manufacturing costs for fixed assets
    Total output
Raw materials and supplies, purchased goods consumed in sale
    Gross profit
Income from profit transfer agreements
Income from trade investments
Income from other long-term investments
Other interest and similar income
Income from the retirement and the appraisal of fixed assets
Income from the cancellation of lump allowances
Income from the cancellation of overstated reserves
Other income (of which . . . is extraordinary)
Income from loss transfer agreements
    Total income

Wages and salaries
Social taxes
Expenses for pension plans and relief
Depreciation and amortization of fixed assets and investments
Depreciation and amortization of finance investments
Losses by deduction or on the retirement of current assets
Losses on the retirement of fixed assets and investments
Interest and similar expenses
Taxes (on income and net assets, and other)
Losses arising from loss transfer agreements
Other expenses
Profits transferable to parent company under profit transfer agreement
    Profit or loss for the period
Profit or loss brought forward from the preceding year
Release of reserves
Amounts appropriated to reserves out of profit of the period
    Accumulated net profit/loss

Source: American Institute of Certified Public Accountants, *Professional Accounting in 30 Countries* (New York: AICPA, 1975), pp. 350-51, 630, 750-53.

Extraordinary profits and losses are usually shown separately on the income statement. However, the definition varies among countries. In a number of countries, the early definition outlined in the U.S. APB Opinion no. 9 in 1966 has been adopted. The change to a stress on the criteria of "unusual nature" and "infrequency of occurrence" as specified in APB Opinion no. 30 in 1973 has not yet been universally adopted. Until an internationally defined standard is established, the many variations in income statement presentation will continue to plague the investment analyst's interpretation of a company's results of operations.

Funds Statement

In the United States, a third financial statement has become basic to the report package required for complete presentation of a company's financial position. This third statement is the funds statement, referred to most frequently as the statement of changes in financial position. An illustrative format is presented in Exhibit 12.3.

The statement became a required one in the United States with the promulgation of APB Opinion no. 19 in 1971. It has since been adopted as a required statement in Canada, Peru, and Panama. Furthermore, its use has been recommended in Australia, England, Mexico, and a number of other countries. As the advantages of its adoption become apparent, a universal utilization should evolve.

EXHIBIT 12.3

Illustrative Consolidated Statements of Changes in the Financial Position of a U.S. Company

| | For the Year Ended December 31, | |
	19__	19__
Working capital was provided by		
Operations		
Income before extraordinary items	$....	$....
Depreciation and amortization of fixed and intangible assets	....	....
Deferred federal income taxes	....	....
Deferred receivables	....	....
Funds provided by operations	....	....
Extraordinary items	....	(....)
Increase in long-term debt	....	....
Retirement of property, plant, and equipment	....	....
Decrease in other assets	....	....
Proceeds from exercise of options and warrants and sale of common stock	....	....
Total funds provided	$	$
Working capital was used to		
Purchase property, plant, and equipment	$....	$....
Retire long-term debt	....	—
Increase investments	—	....
Decrease minority equity in consolidated subsidiaries and other noncurrent liabilities	....	....
Increase (decrease in working capital	....	....
Total funds applied	$	$
Components of working capital changed as follows		
Cash	$....	$....
Marketable securities	(....)	....
Notes and trade accounts receivable	....	(....)
Inventories	....	....
Other current assets	....	....
Notes payable and long-term debt	(....)	(....)
Accounts payable and accrued liabilities	....	....
Accrued federal income taxes	(....)	....
Other current liabilities	....	(....)
Increase (decrease)	$	$

Source: American Institute of Certified Public Accountants, *Professional Accounting in 30 Countries* (New York: AICPA, 1975), p. 693.

The Statement of Changes in Shareholders' Equity

Another basic financial statement is emerging, particularly in the United States: the statement of changes in shareholders' equity.[7] An example is presented as Exhibit 12.4; it is a comprehensive illustration of changes in a number of shareholders' equity accounts. In this case, the statement shows the changes in the retained earnings, paid-in capital, preferred legal capital, common share legal capital, and treasury stock accounts. A statement presenting all changes in shareholders' equity accounts may be particularly important for the international investor who may not be familiar with all the various types of equity capital accounts. The statutory and legal reserve accounts discussed in Chapter 9, for example, may be strange to American investors.

The major advantage of the separate statement is, then, that it presents a simple, perspicuous analysis of changes in the investor's own equity interest in the corporation. Another advantage is that it may aid in synchronizing the worldwide reporting of equity changes. The statement could replace the combined statement of earnings and retained earnings as utilized in some countries. Such a combined statement tends to obstruct the comprehensibility of the income statement portion. Since the income statement is evolving as a required basic statement, it should stand alone. Further, a comprehensive statement of changes in shareholders' equity would alleviate the need to present more than one equity statement—for example, a separate statement for retained earnings and a statement for capital surplus. Separate statements of retained earnings are normally presented with the annual financial statements in many countries.

Other Disclosures

Besides the financial statements, other disclosures may be required. For example, there may be a disclosure of the effects of post-balance sheet events which substantially alter the reader's interpretation of the financial position of the enterprise. The disclosure of significant subsequent events is required in the United States and at least a dozen other countries. The requirements for footnote disclosures vary considerably. The underlying concept that tends to create some demand for footnote disclosures is the materiality concept with its inherent disclosure requirements.

One disclosure requirement that is expected to become universally adopted is the disclosure of basic accounting policies. Policy disclosure will aid the financial statement reader in the interpretation of operational results and financial position. A secondary effect of establishing a disclosure of accounting policies is that it will reveal any unique accounting practices. Complete disclosure hopefully will eventually lead to a rather universal concept as to the fairness of financial statement presentation.

EXHIBIT 12.4

Illustrative Statement of Shareowner's Equity

	4½ Percent Cumulative Preferred Stock, $100 Par Value	Common Stock, $1 Par Value	Additional Paid-in Capital	Retained Earnings	Treasury Common Stock	Total Shareowners' Equity
Balance at December 31, 1973	$1,680,000	$25,528,000	$171,999,000	$377,510,000	($73,561,000)	$503,156,000
Net earnings for the year 1974	—	—	—	80,801,000	—	80,801,000
Cash dividends declared						
Preferred stock	—	—	—	(63,000)	—	(63,000)
Common stock	—	—	—	(27,755,000)	—	(27,755,000)
Stock options exercised	—	31,000	384,000	(416,000)	755,000	754,000
Preferred stock retired	(1,150,000)	—	—	—	—	(1,150,000)
Shares issued in merger	—	—	—	(3,286,000)	31,197,000	27,911,000
Balance at December 31, 1974	530,000	25,559,000	172,383,000	426,791,000	(41,609,000)	583,654,000
Net earnings for the year 1975	—	—	—	55,367,000	—	55,367,000
Cash dividends declared						
Preferred stock	—	—	—	(18,000)	—	(18,000)
Common stock	—	—	—	(30,583,000)	—	(30,583,000)
Stock options exercised	—	86,000	1,067,000	(704,000)	1,656,000	2,105,000
Preferred stock retired	(530,000)	—	—	(530,000)	—	(530,000)
Adjustment of shares issued in merger	—	—	—	197,000	(928,000)	(731,000)
Balance at December 31, 1975	$ —	$25,645,000	$173,450,000	$451,050,000	($40,881,000)	$609,264,000

Source: Martin Marietta Corp., *1975 Annual Report* (Rockville, Md.), p. 27.

REPORTING STANDARDS

A fairness in financial statement presentation depends not only on full disclosure but also on high standards of auditing and professional competence. Fairness and truth in public financial reporting is possible only through respect for and trust in the professional accountant and auditor. The trust is fulfilled through the mechanism of the certified auditor's report.

Audit Certification

In practically every developed and developing country, some type of law or regulatory provision requires regular submission of financial statements to certain governmental bodies, regulatory agencies, or similar institutions. Further, for corporations with stocks listed on official securities exchanges, regulations require submission of the financial statements to the shareholders, too. In most cases, such submitted financial statements must be certified or otherwise attested to by a qualified auditor.

The form of the certification varies. The most prevalent type of audit report is the short-form report used in the United States. The form was approved by members of the Inter-American Accounting Conference at a meeting held in Argentina in 1965. Thus, the short-form report has widespread adoption in most of the Western Hemisphere.

In other countries, the audit report form varies from a very elaborate long-form report used in Germany to a signature-only report in Spain. The second most prevalent type of audit report is the certification as to fairness and truth in accordance with specified regulatory acts. Examples of such reports, along with a sample U.S. short-form report, are presented in Exhibit 12.5. Slight variations of the "true and fair view" report used in New Zealand can be found in the United Kingdom, South Africa, Switzerland, Sweden, and other countries that have had some British influence. The simplistic form used in Denmark also is used in a few other countries. Whether the short-form report used in many countries is adopted in lieu of the legalistic "true and fair" attestation is a controversial issue in developed countries.

Professional Competence

The certification or attestation must normally be by a qualified, registered accountant. Just as one finds variations in the qualifications necessary for certification among the states in the United States, so also are there variations among countries. Sanctioned requirements include some combination of practical experience, formal education, successful examination, and institute or

EXHIBIT 12.5

Illustrative Audit Report Formats

United States

In our opinion, the aforementioned financial statements present fairly the financial position of X Company at December 31, 19_, and the results of its operations and the changes in its financial position for the year then ended, in conformity with generally accepted accounting principles applied on a basis consistent with that of the preceding year.

We have examined the balance sheet of X Company as of December 31, 19_, and the related statements of income and retained earnings and changes in financial position for the year then ended. Our examination was made in accordance with generally accepted auditing standards, and accordingly included such tests of the accounting records and such other auditing procedures as we considered necessary in the circumstances.

New Zealand

We have obtained all the information and explanations that we have required. In our opinion, proper books of account have been kept by the company so far as appears from our examination of those books. In our opinion, according to the best of our information and the explanations given to us and as shown by the said books, the balance sheet and the profit and loss accounts are properly drawn up so as to give respectively a true and fair view of the state of the company's affairs as at (date) _____ and the results of its business for the year ended on that date.

According to such information and explanations the accounts, the balance sheet, and the profit and loss account give the information required by the Companies Act of 1955 in the manner so required.

Switzerland

As auditor(s) of your company, I (we) have examined the accounts for the year ended _____ in accordance with the provisions of the law.

I (we) have come to the conclusion that
—the balance sheet and profit and loss account are in agreement with the books
—the books of accounts have been properly kept
—the financial position and the results of operations are presented in accordance with the principles of evaluation prescribed by the law and the requirements of the statutes.

Based on the result of my (our) examination, I (we) recommend that the accounts submitted to you be approved.

I (we) further confirm that the proposal(s) of the board of directors for the disposal of the available profits is (are) in agreement with the law and the statutes.

Denmark

The above profit and loss account and balance sheet that I have examined are in accordance with the books of the company.

Source: American Institute of Certified Public Accountants, *Professional Accounting in 30 Countries* (New York: AICPA, 1975), pp. 177, 426, 585-86, 653-54.

statutory registration.[3] Needless to say, within the requirements, such as experience and formal training, variations also will always exist.

In most cases, the financial statements of corporations with shares listed on an official securities exchange must have an attestation by a certified, chartered, or registered public accountant. Other corporation financial statements may be attested to by accountants with lower minimum qualifications, those similar to the registered (noncertified) public accountants in some states in the United States.

Auditing Standards

To attain a high level of standards in certification, the auditor must not only have a professional competence but also must exert diligence and integrity in performing the audit. This means that the auditor must use substantive auditing procedures before the certification can be given. Though auditing procedures are required in most countries, the extent and thoroughness of the audit tests are not always at the high level that one might expect from the reading of the short-form audit report.

The lack of inventory observation or receivables confirmation is quite common in most countries. In a few countries, such as Belgium and Italy, there also is no internal control review nor direct confirmation of bank balances. Nevertheless, the auditor does testify to the accuracy of the financial statements as derived from the company's accounts. No doubt, the standardization of audit tests and procedures seems necessary for certification of reports for companies with shares listed on international securities exchanges.

Importance of High Standards in the International Investment Arena

The movement of international investments among the world's citizens is increasing. The increase is in the amount of direct investments among countries—that is, more than just movements of unilateral investments from developed countries to the developing nations. There are movements of investments among the developed countries, too.

The movement in international direct investments has caused a demand for exchanges of investments in a secondary market, whether through securities exchanges, in the over-the-counter market, or in private negotiations. For the exchanges in investment to take place, there must be some understanding as to the intrinsic values, the proper exchange prices, of the investments. This understanding can best be monitored through the review of the financial positions and results of operations of the enterprises involved. Indeed, the international investor is demanding the authentication of financial statements on which trust can be based for the negotiations in the investment exchange price. High levels of professional competence and reporting standards are expected if these international investment exchanges are to be handled in a mutually understanding, trustful manner.

NOTES

1. In addition to the references listed in note 1 of Chapter 9, see Joseph P. Cummings, "Beware of the Pitfalls in Foreign Financial Statements," *PMM & Co. World* 6, no. 1 (Winter 1972): 45-47, and I.N.S. Lathom-Sharp, "International Variations in Presentation and Certification of Accounts," *The Accountant* 165, no. 5040 (July 22, 1971): 124-26.

2. Norlin G. Rueschhoff, "The Next Basic Financial Statement: The Statement of Shareholders' Equity," *The New York Certified Public Accountant* 41, no. 12 (January 1971): 887-90.

3. Cesar A. Salas, "Accounting Education and Practice in Spanish Latin America," *The International Journal of Accounting* 3, no. 1 (Fall 1967): 67-85.

13

THE INTERNATIONAL
ACCOUNTING HORIZON

As international trade and investment multiplies, accounting's international dimension broadens. As more and more business enterprises become multinational in nature, international financial reporting becomes more important as the tool of communication among traders, entrepreneurs, financiers, and investors.

The professional responsibilities of the public accountant and management accountant, however, are no longer limited strictly to fiscal matters. Social accounting concepts have extended the accountant's responsibility to evaluation of social programs and reporting of social, environmental, and political contributions to society. Thus, the accountant has a broader audience of report readers. Further, accountants have been employed in new arenas, among which there may be a significant future effort in the area of macroaccounting.

At the same time, variations are evolving in accounting principles, audit practices, financial statement presentations, and professional standards. If accounting reports are to become a universal means of communication, action must be taken to harmonize the worldwide efforts to meet the international users' needs.

THE INTERNATIONALIZATION PROCESS AND ITS ACTIVITIES

Congresses of Accountants

An international accounting effort has developed through the convening of ten international congresses of accountants, as follows:

Congress	Site	Year
First	St. Louis	1904
Second	Amsterdam	1926
Third	New York	1929
Fourth	London	1933
Fifth	Berlin	1938
Sixth	London	1952
Seventh	Amsterdam	1957
Eighth	New York	1962
Ninth	Paris	1967
Tenth	Sydney	1972

The eleventh, scheduled for Munich in 1977, has the theme "Accounting and Auditing in One World."

The congresses did not have a linking organization until the 1970s. However, the 1967 congress gave major impetus to the internationalization process, as exemplified by the following quote:[1]

> Almost all the international and national authors are in favor of the harmonization of accounting and auditing principles, and some even considered that this harmonization is essential and really urgent. The rare exceptions to this opinion come from those authors who have taken harmonization as meaning standardization, uniformity or unification, which is obviously out of the question.

These were the remarks of F. M. Richard, president of the Ninth International Congress of Accountants (Paris, 1967). During the discussions held at this congress, influential professional accounts were inspired by harmonization efforts. Such efforts led to the formation of an international working party, comprising 14 individuals from a variety of countries. The ad hoc objective of this committee was to review the part played by the periodic international congresses in the continuing and progressive development of accounting thought and understanding and, in that context, to consider the scope and frequency of such congresses and their objectives.

After three meetings, the working party in December 1971 issued its final report, promoting harmonization. Among its recommendations was a proposal to form the International Coordination Committee for the Accountancy Profession (ICCAP). Steps taken at the Tenth International Congress in Sydney in October 1972 led to ICCAP's formation in November 1972.

The Forming of a Harmonization Committee

The 11 members of ICCAP, representing Australia, Canada, Germany, France, India, Japan, Mexico, the Netherlands, Philippines, the United Kingdom, and the United States, took a giant stride toward harmonization at its first plenary session at Dusseldorf in April 1973 by its decision to form the International Accounting Standards Committee. By June 1973 the IASC constitution was formalized and signed by nine representatives of member accounting institutes.

Though part of ICCAP, IASC has autonomy to promulgate accounting standards to be observed in the presentation of audited accounts and financial statements. The committee's objectives are to formulate and publish international accounting standards and to promote their worldwide acceptance and observance. To assure success, the founders agree to support the IASC objectives. Specifically, the member institutes of IASC have promised to support the standards promulgated by the committee and use their best endeavors to ensure that published financial statements and auditors' reports indicate compliance with the standards. If the international standards differ from local regulations, the financial statements and auditors' report are to indicate the respects in which the international accounting standards have not been observed. If the audit reports are not in consonance with the standards and disclosure is not properly presented in the financial statements, the member organizations are obligated to take appropriate action, which may be of a disciplinary nature to assure compliance. At its first meeting in June 1973, the IASC selected topics for its first three international accounting standards: disclosure of accounting policies, valuation of inventories, and consolidated financial statements. The committee agreed that the first subject should be disclosure of accounting policies, which would have the advantage of clarifying the policies currently pursued in different countries throughout the world.

With consideration given geographical circumstances and the associated problems of travel and communication, steering committees were established. With the help of the IASC secretariat, the steering committees, prepared the exposure drafts on the first three standards, for deliberation by all IASC committee members at the regular meetings. Through this process, exposure drafts were issued in 1974 and the three standards have been subsequently finalized for implementation by international accountants.

International Accounting Study Groups

An important step in the harmonization process was the establishment of the Accountants International Study Group (AISG). Its publications have been used as background research for the establishment of international standards.

The AISG consists of representatives from the Institute of Chartered Accountants in England and Wales, the Canadian Institute of Chartered Accountants, and the AICPA. The study group met for the first time in February 1967, and now meets twice a year. Its purpose is to study common areas of practice; it issues its publications through the three member institutes. The publications of other regional groups such as the Groupe d'Etude of the Common Market and the Inter-American Accounting Conference also are contributory to the international effort.

The Early Results of the Internationalization Process

Accounting was never established as a national discipline but emerged as a universal art. But somehow through the ages national characteristics have seemed to limit the universal applicability of the results of the accounting process.

There is a need to review the development of the accounting process. Such a review is being accomplished through the efforts of the international study groups. There also is a need to propose new horizons to again reestablish a universal art of accounting. The harmonization effort is being tackled by the IASC and the ICCAP. Thus, these groups have spurred the internationalization process, and their activities will aid in establishing a perspective for launching new goals in the international accounting horizon.

THE NEED FOR A HOLISTIC PERSPECTIVE

The Establishment of Worldwide Objectives

At the Ninth International Congress of Accountants (Paris, 1967), T. K. Cowan recommended the formulation and acceptance of a statement of broad accounting objectives, as follows:[2]

1. that it be recognized that the primary addressees of the external accounting reports of the businesses are the stockholders (owners);
2. that the balance sheet be a statement of the resources entrusted to management;
3. that an income statement should show primarily the income which arose during the period covered, from the viewpoint of the resources of the undertaking with a subsequent adjustment for special practice such as the effective price changes; and
4. that the basic objective in preparation be truth, and in presentation, fairness.

It is interesting to note that, in the issuance of International Accounting Standard no. 1 and its accompanying preface, certain of these broad objectives have been adopted.[3] The stockholders of public companies are identified as the primary report users. Although the specific definitions of a balance sheet and an income statement are not given, those two statements, as well as other statements and notes, are included in the overall definition of financial statements. Thus, the harmonization effort has begun; indeed, the lid on the harmonization pot has been lifted, with thoughts and efforts flowing profusely. If the international standards derived therefrom can be properly streamlined to the user needs under a holistic approach, true harmonization will prevail.

Approaches to Worldwide Objectives

The challenge is to establish a holistic approach to accounting objectives. There are at least three approaches by which such a holistic objective may be achieved: the legalistic, the situationistic, and the principled. All three are in existence today in some form.

The legalistic approach is exemplified by the company statements found in the British Commonwealth countries and in the Germanic countries. One can identify the approach by viewing the auditors' reports given in some countries. Some of the reports merely state that the financial statements are prepared in accordance with the law.

The accounting objective also has been fulfilled through situationism. In fact a situationistic approach is common throughout the world. It involves a loose type of structure that develops principles according to the situation. However, over time certain principles become prevalent under specific situations, and standard principles become generally accepted. This is the avenue that is prevalent in the United States.

Eventually a principled approach should receive attention. Such an approach would require that established principles be in consonance with a common, a total, objective. Thus, the accountant should take a holistic view: the application of theory should be based on total awareness of user needs.

Attaining the Holistic Perspective

One way to achieve the goals of a principled total approach is to establish a holistic simulation model. Such a model would help accountants to anticipate the effects of new accounting principles on the firm and the total economy before such principles are promulgated; principles affect economic decisions.

The simulation model must include the simple relationships of a national economy and its relationships with another economy. Understanding of the whole can be just as complete with one or two breakdowns as it can with multiple breakdowns. For example, a practitioner has related that the theory that he had learned in a university advanced accounting course on how to consolidate financial statements is sufficient for him to consolidate 250 subsidiaries even though the examples that he had learned at the university level were only for a parent and a subsidiary. Again, this indicates that a simple structure is all that is necessary.

The mechanics of an accounting model have already been begun. In a 1975 publication, a proposed balance sheet and income statement is outlined for the national economy.[4] What also is needed then is a setup of entities that represent the total within the economy. There might be, for example, one industrial corporation, one bank, one service company, and a small governmental unit.

The effects of accounting theories on the financial data presented on financial statements also has already been tried. For example, an elaborate system of work papers was devised for the translation problem.[5] The extension of the analysis to the social effects of different principles on the total economy and environment is appropriate under a holistic approach. In this age of rapid communication and transportation, the goal of a harmonized set of international financial reporting standards of all resource changes is indeed forseeable on the horizon.

NOTES

1. F. M. Richard, *New Horizons of Accounting* (Paris: International Congress of Accountants, 1967), p. 11.

2. T. K. Cowan, "Harmonization of Accounting Principles," in *New Horizons of Accounting* (Paris: International Congress of Accountants, 1967), p. 156.

3. International Accounting Standards Committee, *Disclosure of Accounting Policies*, and *Preface to Statements of International Accounting Standards*, International Accounting Standard no. 1 (London: IASC, 1974).

4. Arthur Andersen & Co., *Sound Financial Reporting in the Public Sector* (Chicago: Arthur Andersen, 1975), pp. 7-21.

5. See Financial Accounting Standards Board, *An Analysis of Issues Related to Accounting For Foreign Currency Translation, FASB Discussion Memorandum* (Stamford, 1974), p. x.

APPENDIX:
ILLUSTRATIVE CONSOLIDATED
FINANCIAL STATEMENT

UNITED STATES GOVERNMENT
June 30, 1974 and 1973

For purposes of illustration, we have collected financial information currently available in several publications of the United States Government and have used this information as a basis for preparing consolidated financial statements of the United States Government in conventional format as of June 30, 1974 and 1973, and for the years then ended.

The amounts reflected in the following illustrative financial statements and notes thereto have not been audited by Arthur Andersen & Co., and accordingly, we do not express an opinion on them. Even though these financial statements may not be complete and accurate in all respects, they do provide the necessary background for discussion of some of the issues involved.

This appendix is reprinted from pages 7-21 of *Sound Financial Reporting in the Public Sector: A Prerequisite to Fiscal Responsibility*, prepared by Arthur Andersen & Co., Chicago, Ill., 1975.

149

UNITED STATES GOVERNMENT
ILLUSTRATIVE CONSOLIDATED BALANCE SHEET
(Unaudited) (Notes 1 and 2)
JUNE 30, 1974 AND 1973

ASSETS

	Millions	
	1974	1973
CASH AND CASH EQUIVALENTS	$ 18,127	$ 22,797
GOLD, at official rate (Note 3)	11,567	10,410
RECEIVABLES (net of allowances):		
Accounts	5,490	4,859
Taxes (Note 4)	14,960	12,844
Loans (Note 5)	65,836	62,985
	86,286	80,688
INVENTORIES, at cost (Note 6):		
Military and strategic system supplies	28,019	25,173
Stockpiled materials and commodities	11,526	12,693
Other materials and supplies	11,026	12,012
	50,571	49,878
PROPERTY AND EQUIPMENT, at cost:		
Land (Note 7)	6,686	6,415
Buildings, structures and facilities (Note 8)	88,649	86,129
Strategic and tactical military assets (Note 9)	119,913	117,670
Nonmilitary equipment (Note 9)	39,708	37,3/7
Construction in progress	19,400	17,169
Other	2,118	1,848
	276,474	266,608
Less—Accumulated depreciation (Note 10)	129,000	122,000
	147,474	144,608
DEFERRED CHARGES AND OTHER ASSETS	15,297	15,369
	$329,322	$323,750

LIABILITIES AND DEFICIT

	Millions	
	1974	1973
FEDERAL DEBT (Note 11):		
Gross debt outstanding	$ 486,247	$ 468,426
Less—Intragovernmental holdings—		
Trust funds	(129,745)	(114,852)
Federal Reserve	(80,649)	(75,182)
Other	(10,449)	(10,529)
Debt outstanding with the public	265,404	267,863
Less—Unamortized discount	2,506	2,243
	262,898	265,620
FEDERAL RESERVE LIABILITIES:		
Federal Reserve Notes outstanding	64,263	58,754
Deposits of member banks	26,760	25,506
Other	2,286	1,725
	93,309	85,985
ACCOUNTS PAYABLE AND ACCRUED LIABILITIES:		
Accounts payable	32,491	30,757
Accrued interest, annual leave and other	11,187	11,819
Deferred revenue	6,734	6,565
	50,412	49,141
OTHER LIABILITIES	18,991	19,836
RETIREMENT AND DISABILITY BENEFITS (Note 12):		
Civil Service	108,000	97,000
Military	80,380	70,950
Veterans	110,980	110,850
	299,360	278,800
ACCRUED SOCIAL SECURITY (Note 13)	416,020	340,930
CONTINGENCIES (Note 14)		
Total liabilities	1,140,990	1,040,312
LESS—ACCUMULATED DEFICIT	811,668	716,562
	$ 329,322	$ 323,750

The accompanying notes are an integral part of this balance sheet.

UNITED STATES GOVERNMENT

ILLUSTRATIVE CONSOLIDATED STATEMENT OF REVENUES AND EXPENSES

(Unaudited) (Notes 1 and 2)

FOR THE YEARS ENDED JUNE 30, 1974 AND 1973

	Millions	
	1974	1973
REVENUES:		
Individual income taxes	$118,952	$103,246
Social Security and unemployment taxes and retirement contributions	76,780	64,541
Corporate income taxes	40,736	37,588
Excise taxes	16,844	16,260
Estate and gift taxes	5,035	4,917
Outer continental shelf rents and royalties	6,748	3,956
Other (Note 3)	6,539	4,970
Total revenues	271,634	235,478
EXPENSES (including transfer payments):		
National defense—		
Military personnel	23,728	23,246
Operations and maintenance	27,698	24,980
Research and development	8,582	8,157
Depreciation (Note 10)	11,100	10,800
Other	1,371	3,091
	72,479	70,274
Other operating expenses, including depreciation of $2,100 million in 1974 and $2,000 million in 1973 (Note 10)	41,982	36,328
Grants-in-aid, primarily to state and local governments	41,500	40,400
Transfer payments to individuals—		
Income security, including retirement, unemployment and Social Security payments made	69,381	60,373
Health care	11,300	9,000
Veterans' benefits and services	10,400	9,700
Other	6,900	4,800
	97,981	83,873
Noncash provision for retirement and disability benefits—		
Social Security (Note 13)	75,090	63,670
Other (Note 12)	20,560	13,360
	95,650	77,030
Interest expense (net of interest income)	17,148	14,146
Total expenses	366,740	322,051
EXCESS OF EXPENSES OVER REVENUES (Note 15)	$ 95,106	$ 86,573

The accompanying notes are an integral part of this statement.

UNITED STATES GOVERNMENT

ILLUSTRATIVE CONSOLIDATED STATEMENT OF CHANGES IN CASH AND CASH EQUIVALENTS

(Unaudited) (Notes 1 and 2)

FOR THE YEAR ENDED JUNE 30, 1974

		Millions
SOURCES OF CASH:		
Excess of expenses over revenues		$(95,106)
Add (deduct) items not affecting cash—		
Depreciation (Note 10)		13,200
Noncash provision for retirement and disability benefit expense (Notes 12 and 13)		95,650
Revenue attributable to change in gold valuation (Note 3)		(1,157)
Increase in accrued corporate income taxes receivable		(2,116)
Effect of other accrual adjustments (net)		(151)
Cash provided by operations		10,320
Increase in Federal Reserve liabilities		7,324
Total sources of cash		17,644
USES OF CASH:		
Decrease in net Federal debt—		
Increase in gross debt outstanding	$17,821	
Less—Increase in intragovernmental holdings:		
Trust funds	14,893	
Federal Reserve	5,467	
Other	(80)	
	20,280	
Decrease in debt outstanding with the public	2,459	
Increase in unamortized debt discount	263	2,722
Additions to property and equipment		16,066
Increase in loans receivable		2,851
Net change in other assets and liabilities		675
Total uses of cash		22,314
DECREASE IN CASH		(4,670)
CASH AT BEGINNING OF YEAR		22,797
CASH AT END OF YEAR		$ 18,127

The accompanying notes are an integral part of this statement.

UNITED STATES GOVERNMENT

Notes to Illustrative Consolidated Financial Statements
(Unaudited)
June 30, 1974 and 1973

1. SOURCES OF DATA

The United States Government does not have a centralized accounting system which would furnish data necessary for the preparation of consolidated financial statements on an accrual basis. The asset and liability amounts included herein were obtained from several sources within the Government. For some agencies, numbers purporting to reflect the same items were available from more than one source and differed as to amount. In such instances, the sources which appeared to be the most reliable were used.

2. PRINCIPLES OF CONSOLIDATION

The accompanying financial statements include the accounts of all significant agencies and funds included in the Unified Budget of the United States Government, plus those of the traditional "off budget" agencies and the Federal Reserve System. Government-sponsored enterprises such as Federal Land Banks have been excluded because they are privately owned. Amounts reflected are as of June 30, 1974 and 1973, except for the Federal Reserve System, which reports on a calendar-year basis and for which December 31, 1973 and 1972, amounts were used. Intragovernmental assets, liabilities and revenue/expense items of significance have been eliminated in consolidation.

The Federal Reserve System (which operates independently from the Executive and Legislative branches of the Government) has been included in the accompanying financial statements because of the interrelationships between the Federal Reserve System and the Treasury.

a. A large portion of the Federal debt is held by Federal Reserve banks.
b. Virtually all of the gold has been "pledged" to the Federal Reserve banks in return for Treasury demand deposits.
c. The net income of the Federal Reserve System is transferred annually to the Treasury.
d. In the event of liquidation, after capital contributed by member banks is returned, residuals of Federal Reserve banks would be transferred to the Treasury.

The effect of including the Federal Reserve System in the consolidated balance sheet as of June 30, 1974, is summarized below.

	Millions
Increase total assets	$ 3,089
Reduce Federal debt	$(80,649)
Eliminate gold certificate liability	(11,460)
Add Federal Reserve Notes	64,263
Add deposits of member banks	26,760
Increase other liability accounts	2,286
	1,200
Reduce deficit	1,889
	$ 3,089

154

Government trust funds have been included in the accompanying consolidated financial statements. This reporting has been adopted because the trust funds are included in the Unified Budget and because the assets in such funds are almost exclusively Federal debt securities. In substance, the Government trust funds serve as segregated accounts for specific purposes rather than as trusts.

3. GOLD

Gold has been recorded at the official rate established by Congress ($42.22 per ounce at June 30, 1974, and $38.00 per ounce at June 30, 1973). Although the free market rate for gold is currently much higher, a different rate was not used because (1) the official rate is the basis upon which the Treasury uses the gold as security to increase its demand deposits with the Federal Reserve (most of the gold has been utilized in this way) and (2) it is not possible to determine what effect sales of the Treasury's gold would have on the free market price and, therefore, what alternative value would be appropriate. If the free market rate as of June 30, 1974, of $144.50 per ounce had been used, the aggregate carrying value of gold would have been $39,586 million.

The effect of the change in the official rate for gold between June 30, 1973, and June 30, 1974, is reflected as revenue of the Government in the accompanying consolidated statement of revenues and expenses because such a valuation increase allows the Treasury to increase its cash balances.

4. TAXES RECEIVABLE

The total for taxes receivable includes $5.0 billion (net) for delinquent taxes owed and $10.0 billion of accrued corporate income taxes receivable as of June 30, 1974; the comparable amounts as of June 30, 1973, were $5.1 billion and $7.7 billion, respectively. No accrual has been made for individual income taxes because of the payroll withholding system. Also, assessed tax deficiencies pending settlement have not been included in receivables because the ultimate settlement value is indeterminable.

5. LOANS RECEIVABLE

Interest rates and loan repayment terms vary considerably for outstanding loans, with rates ranging from zero to 12.0% and terms from as short as 90 days to well over 40 years. The longer terms and lower rates generally apply to loans to foreign governments. Outstanding balances and allowances for losses have been recorded as reported by the various lending agencies. No attempt has been made to evaluate collectibility or the adequacy of the allowances for losses. Loans outstanding are summarized below by major classification of borrower.

	Millions	
Classification	1974	1973
Business entities	$20,434	$17,200
Students, farmers and other individuals	22,502	21,264
Foreign	19,794	21,588
State and local governments	2,123	1,838
Other	2,513	2,251
	67,366	64,141
Less—Allowances for losses	1,530	1,156
	$65,836	$62,985

6. INVENTORIES

Inventories include nondepreciable personal property and are generally stated at cost. The major components of inventory are summarized below.

Classification	Millions	
	1974	1973
Military and strategic system supplies—		
Ammunition	$ 9,387	$ 6,944
Materials related to missile, air and weapons systems	11,293	11,167
Repair parts for weapons and vehicles	2,545	2,425
Excess materials awaiting disposition	2,354	2,862
Miscellaneous	2,440	1,775
	28,019	25,173
Stockpiled materials and commodities—		
Nuclear materials	6,599	6,611
Metals and like materials	4,417	5,595
Helium	510	487
	11,526	12,693
Other materials and supplies—		
Electric, industrial and petroleum supplies	4,094	4,141
Clothing, subsistence and general supplies	1,936	1,799
Excess materials awaiting disposition	2,190	2,333
Miscellaneous	524	1,395
Subtotal—Department of Defense	8,744	9,668
Agencies other than Department of Defense	2,282	2,344
	11,026	12,012
	$50,571	$49,878

The inventory accounts do not include the weapons stockpile of the Atomic Energy Commission, since the extent of this inventory is classified information.

7. LAND

Land owned by the Government as of June 30, 1974, is summarized below by predominant usage.

Usage	Acres (Millions)	Cost (Millions)
Forest and wildlife	503.2	$ 497
Grazing	163.5	26
Parks and historic sites	25.1	477
Alaska oil and gas reserves	23.0	—
Military (except airfields)	18.1	314
Flood control and navigation	8.0	3,256
Reclamation and irrigation	7.0	305
Industrial	2.9	204
Airfields	2.3	203
Power development and distribution	1.5	272
Other	5.9	979
	760.5	6,533
Outside United States	.6	153
	761.1	$6,686

The outer continental shelf and other offshore land are not included above.

The Government owns approximately 33.5% of the total acreage of the United States, or 761 million acres (of which 352 million acres are located in Alaska). This total includes 704 million acres of public domain land (land vested in the United States by virtue of its sovereignty).

Cost represents cost to the Government, except that the cost of land acquired through donation, exchange, devise, forfeiture or judicial process is estimated at amounts the Government would have had to pay for the properties if purchased at the date of acquisition by the Government. Public domain land is included at no cost.

A committee of the House of Representatives reported as of June 30, 1972, that the estimated current value of the 704 million acres of public domain land was approximately $29.9 billion. No similar reports are available estimating current values for other land, mineral resources or the outer continental shelf.

8. BUILDINGS, STRUCTURES AND FACILITIES

This category includes all real property owned by the Government except land. Approximately $36 billion of the total at June 30, 1974, and $35 billion at June 30, 1973, reflects the acquisition cost of buildings, whereas the balance includes the costs of acquiring or erecting dams, utility systems, monuments, roads and bridges. The following table summarizes the buildings, structures and facilities reported.

Agency or Department	Millions 1974	1973
Air Force	$16,738	$16,859
Army—		
Corps of Engineers	14,309	13,752
Other	12,105	11,898
Navy	12,168	11,839
Interior	9,018	8,885
Tennessee Valley Authority	4,769	4,490
Atomic Energy Commission	4,171	4,061
Agriculture	3,035	2,914
NASA	2,471	2,475
General Services Administration	2,373	2,315
Other	7,492	6,641
	$88,649	$86,129

9. DEPRECIABLE PERSONAL PROPERTY

Depreciable personal property has been divided into two categories to split out that portion which relates solely to defense of the nation from that which may have nonmilitary applications. The assets are recorded at acquisition cost and include only those which are currently in use or in usable condition. The major components of each category are summarized below.

Classification	Millions	
	1974	1973
Strategic and tactical military assets—		
Aircraft and related equipment	$ 51,032	$ 49,891
Ships and service craft	36,268	36,081
Combat and tactical vehicles	16,923	18,324
Missiles and related equipment	9,746	9,255
Weapons	1,091	509
Other (primarily ground support)	4,853	3,610
	$119,913	$117,670

Classification	Millions	
	1974	1973
Nonmilitary equipment—Department of Defense—		
Industrial plant equipment	$14,028	$13,833
Communication and electronics	4,123	3,997
Vehicles	2,149	2,168
Other	1,435	459
	21,735	20,457
Atomic Energy Commission	5,814	5,548
Maritime Administration	1,538	1,729
Tennessee Valley Authority	1,348	1,206
U. S. Postal Service	1,158	984
Other agencies	8,115	7,453
	$39,708	$37,377

10. DEPRECIATION

Most Government agencies do not depreciate property and equipment. Accumulated depreciation as of June 30, 1974 and 1973, for such agencies was estimated based on available information; reported amounts were used for those agencies (e.g., AEC and TVA) which do depreciate property and equipment. The methods used to arrive at accumulated depreciation for the major categories of property and equipment are described below.

Buildings—Acquisition dates and original costs were obtained for all buildings owned by the Government as of June 30, 1974, and accumulated depreciation was determined based on the number of years each building had been owned.

Structures and Facilities—Net additions in this category were obtained for the last 21 years, and accumulated depreciation was computed under the assumptions that the balance as of June 30, 1953, was one-half depreciated as of that date, that such balance would be depreciated evenly over the remaining one-half of the estimated useful life for this classification, and that there were no sales or retirements since 1953 for this category.

Military Assets and Nonmilitary Equipment—Net additions by major category were obtained for the past 20 years for the Department of Defense. Budget outlays for major equipment purchases were compared to net addition amounts to arrive at estimated percentages for retirements, and the available information and estimates were extended to cover all assets within these categories to arrive at gross addition and retirement figures by year. Estimated useful lives were then used to determine the remaining undepreciated portions of gross additions.

Depreciation by year was computed on a straight-line basis with no salvage values.

Useful lives were selected for major categories to spread the acquisition costs over the periods during which the average asset in each group could reasonably be expected to be useful at the time of acquisition. The useful lives adopted for agencies for which estimates were required are listed below.

Classification	Life
Buildings, structures and facilities	50 years
Ships and service craft	30 years
Industrial plant equipment	20 years
All other depreciable assets	10 years

Accumulated depreciation balances so computed as of June 30, 1974 and 1973, are shown below by balance sheet classification.

	Millions	
Classification	1974	1973
Buildings, structures and facilities	$ 45,000	$ 43,700
Strategic and tactical military assets	63,500	59,700
Nonmilitary equipment	20,000	18,100
Other	500	500
	$129,000	$122,000

11. FEDERAL DEBT

The gross amount of Federal debt outstanding at June 30, 1974, and June 30, 1973, consisted of the securities summarized below.

	Millions	
Type of Security	1974	1973
Marketable—		
Treasury bills	$105,019	$100,060
Treasury notes	128,419	117,840
Treasury bonds	33,137	45,071
	266,575	262,971
Nonmarketable—		
U. S. Savings bonds	61,921	59,418
Foreign series	25,011	28,524
Government account series (special issues related to specific funds)	115,442	101,738
Other	5,286	4,666
Total Treasury obligations	474,235	457,317
Agency securities	12,012	11,109
	$486,247	$468,426

Maturities of the outstanding marketable securities are reflected in the following table.

Due Within	Millions	
	1974	1973
One year	$139,942	$122,803
One to five years	77,199	88,223
Five to ten years	26,957	31,111
Ten to twenty years	17,403	14,477
Twenty years or longer	5,074	6,357
	$266,575	$262,971

The gross amount of Federal debt outstanding has been reduced by the holdings of entities included in the consolidated financial statements. The largest such reduction reflects the holdings of Government trust funds. Significant trust fund holdings of Federal debt securities are summarized below.

Trust Fund	Millions	
	1974	1973
Social Security Administration—		
Federal old-age and survivors' insurance	$ 37,717	$ 35,501
Federal disability insurance	8,195	7,803
Federal hospital insurance	7,864	4,222
Federal supplementary medical insurance	1,231	700
	55,007	48,226
Civil Service Commission—		
Civil Service retirement and disability	34,331	30,866
Other	1,672	1,468
	36,003	32,334
Department of Labor—Unemployment	12,121	10,957
Department of Transportation—		
Highway	7,599	5,550
Other	878	—
	8,477	5,550
Veterans Administration	7,567	7,428
Federal Deposit Insurance Corporation	5,861	5,636
Other	4,709	4,721
	$129,745	$114,852

Of the debt outstanding with the public at June 30, 1974, and June 30, 1973, approximately $57.7 billion and $60.2 billion, respectively, was held by foreign and international investors.

12. RETIREMENT AND DISABILITY BENEFITS

Liabilities for military retirement benefits and for retirement and disability benefits provided under Civil Service have been recorded, irrespective of whether trust funds exist for the programs, because the liabilities are those of the Government and not of the trust funds and since the covered individuals worked directly for the Government. The recorded amounts are based on the estimated present values of vested benefits, which were derived from the actuarially computed present values of future benefits (as computed by the Government) less the present values of future employee contributions, if any.

The liability for Veterans Administration benefits represents the computed present value of annual benefit payments, which have been estimated by the Government to the year 1999.

The noncash provisions for retirement and disability benefits of $20,560 million for 1974 and $13,360 million for 1973 represent the combined changes in the liabilities for Civil Service, military retirement and veterans' benefits between years.

No attempt has been made to record liabilities for several other Government plans providing future benefits, since the total liabilities for such plans would not be significant in relation to those recorded and certain basic information was not readily available.

13. ACCRUED SOCIAL SECURITY

The Government computes two estimates of future liabilities for Social Security. These estimates are based on a present-value approach, taking into consideration future contributions and benefits which have been established by present laws. Beginning in 1972, benefits are automatically adjusted for changes in the consumer price index. The first estimate, usually referred to as the Official Actuarial Concept, indicates that the excess of benefits to be paid to present and future participants over anticipated receipts for the next seventy-five years on a present-value basis is $1.312 trillion as of June 30, 1974. The second estimate, usually referred to as the Full-Reserve Actuarial Concept, estimates that the excess of benefits to be paid to present participants over contributions by present participants on a present-value basis is $2.460 trillion as of June 30, 1974. This estimate is based on concepts that more closely approximate those used in the private sector.

An accrual for Social Security benefits is reflected in the accompanying financial statements because it appears that such benefits could not be terminated or substantially curtailed without serious social and political implications. Social Security receipts and disbursements are also included in the Unified Budget. Further, in principle, the consolidated financial statements and the accumulated deficit should reflect a liability for the amount of future benefits that will not be covered by future contributions under present law. Under this principle, inclusion of an accrual would seem to be both proper and required. It is recognized that the Social Security Act states that payments should be made only to the extent of the trust funds and that covered individuals who have contributed to the fund have no contractual right to receive benefits; however, this does not negate the need to accrue a liability.

An argument could be made to support the current accrual in full of the estimated present value of the difference between future revenue and benefits, i.e., $2.460 trillion for the Full-Reserve Actuarial Concept. However, it was concluded that a more realistic approach would be to accrue for such amounts over a reasonable future period. In determining such period, recognition was given to the fact that the estimated average period for present participants to contribute revenue under the Full-Reserve Actuarial Concept would approximate 25 to 30 years; further, the

Government amortizes its prior service costs for Civil Service retirement benefits over a thirty-year period, and any period up to 40 years could be used to amortize prior service costs in the private sector. A period of 30 years was used as a reasonable period in this regard for establishing the amount to be accrued.

The estimated amounts by which the present values of future benefits exceed future receipts, determined on an annual basis for the past five years under the Full-Reserve Actuarial Concept, are as follows (in billions): 1970—$415; 1971—$435; 1972—$1,865; 1973—$2,118; and 1974—$2,460. Using the thirty-year period to amortize the increase for each year results in an accrual of $416 billion as of June 30, 1974, and $341 billion as of June 30, 1973, as reflected in the accompanying balance sheet.

The noncash provisions for Social Security benefits of $75,090 million for 1974 and $63,670 million for 1973 represent the changes in accrued Social Security between years.

14. CONTINGENCIES

Several Government agencies insure businesses and individuals against various risks. The amount of insurance coverage in force, representing the maximum contingent exposure of the Government, is summarized below as of June 30, 1974.

Nature of Coverage	Millions
Federal Deposit Insurance Corporation	$ 442,000
Federal Savings and Loan Insurance Corporation	220,000
Housing and Urban Development—Riot Reinsurance	175,000
Atomic Energy Commission	60,000
Other	144,000
	$1,041,000

The Government, under several agencies and programs, guarantees loans made to businesses and individuals by non-Government enterprises, such as commercial banks, and by privately owned, Government-sponsored enterprises, such as Federal Land Banks. These guarantees become assets and/or liabilities of the Government only when the Government is required to honor its guarantees. Loan guarantees in force at June 30, 1974, are summarized below.

Guarantee Related To	Amount Outstanding (Millions)
Federal Housing Administration	$ 97,753
Veterans Administration	27,053
Farm Credit Administration	23,612
Federal Home Loan Bank Board	20,733
Federal National Mortgage Association	25,828
Other	32,583
	$227,562

The annual rental of real property leased throughout the world to the United States Government is approximately $600 million.

15. RECONCILIATION OF BUDGET DEFICIT

The following tabulation reconciles the reported budget deficits for the years ended June 30, 1974 and 1973, to the excess of expenses over revenues reflected for each year in the accompanying statement of revenues and expenses.

	Millions	
	1974	1973
Reported budget deficit (Appendix 1) . .	$ 3,460	$14,300
Add—		
Noncash provisions for retirement and disability benefits	95,650	77,030
Depreciation	13,200	12,800
Net expenses of off budget agencies . .	2,675	607
	111,525	90,437
Deduct—		
Capital outlays	16,066	16,117
Net effects of accrual adjustments . . .	2,267	1,586
Revenue attributable to change in gold valuation	1,157	—
Seigniorage	321	400
Earnings of Federal Reserve	68	61
	19,879	18,164
Excess of expenses over revenues	$ 95,106	$86,573

Accountants International Study Group. *Consolidated Financial Statements.* New York: American Institute of Certified Public Accountants, 1973.

American Institute of Certified Public Accountants, 1973. *The Equity Method of Accounting for Investments in Common Stock, APB Opinion No. 18.* New York: AICPA, 1971.

———. *Audits of Personal Financial Statements.* New York: AICPA, 1968.

———. *Audits of State and Local Governmental Units.* New York: AICPA, 1974.

———. *Professional Accounting in 30 Countries.* New York: AICPA, 1975.

———. *Restatement and Revision of Accounting Research Bulletins,* Accounting Research Bulletin no. 43. New York: AICPA, 1953.

"Are Currency Exchange Costs Nibbling at Your Overseas Profits?" *Business Abroad* 95, no. 2 (February 1970): 14-15.

Arpan, Jeffry S. "International Intracorporate Pricing; Non-American Systems and Views." *Journal of International Business Studies* 3, no. 1 (Spring 1972): 1-18.

Arthur Andersen & Co. *Sound Financial Reporting in the Public Sector.* Chicago: Arthur Andersen, 1975.

Briner, Ernst R. "International Tax Management." *Management Accounting* 54, no. 8 (February 1973): 47-50.

Business International. *Hedging Foreign Exchange Risks,* Management Monograph no. 49. New York: Business International, 1971.

———. *Organizing for International Finance,* Management Monograph no. 35. New York: Business International, 1966.

———. *Solving Accounting Problems for Worldwide Operations.* New York: Business International, 1974.

———. *Solving International Pricing Problems.* New York: Business International, 1965.

Cummings, Joseph P. "Beware of the Pitfalls in Foreign Financial Statements." *PMM & Co. World* 6, no. 1 (Winter 1972): 45-47.

Elliott, C. Willard. "The Lower-of-Cost-and-Market Test for Foreign Inventories." *N.A.A. Bulletin* 46, no. 6 (February 1965): 12-17.

Farrell, Edward L. "Tax Planning and the Multinational Corporation." *Tax Planning,* February 1974, pp. 11-15.

Financial Accounting Standards Board. *An Analysis of Issues Related to Accounting for Foreign Currency Translation, FASB Discussion Memorandum.* Stamford: FASB, 1974.

——. *Accounting and Reporting by Development Stage Enterprises.* Statement of Financial Accounting Standards, no. 7. Stamford: FASB, 1975.

——. *Accounting for the Translation of Foreign Currency Transactions and Foreign Currency Financial Statements.* Statement of Financial Accounting Standards, no. 8. Stamford: FASB, 1975.

Furlong, William R. "How to Eliminate the 'Plugging' of Net Worth for Translated Foreign Currency Financial Statements." *Management Accounting* 49, no. 8 (April 1968): 39-45.

Greene, James, and Michael G. Duerr. *Intercompany Transactions in the Multinational Firm.* New York: National Industrial Conference Board, 1970.

Griffin, Charles H., Thomas H. Williams, and Kermit D. Larson. *Advanced Accounting.* Homewood, Ill.: Richard D. Irwin, 1971.

Haskins and Sells. *International Tax and Business Services—Reporting, Accounting and Business Practices Abroad.* New York: Haskins and Sells, 1972.

Hauworth, William P. "International Accounting Organizations." *The Arthur Andersen Chronicle* 34, no. 3 (July 1974): 92-95.

Holmes, Alan R., and Francis H. Schott. *The New York Foreign Exchange Market.* New York: Federal Reserve Bank: 1965.

Horwitz, Bertrand. *Accounting Controls and Soviet Economic Reforms of 1966.* Evanston, Ill.: American Accounting Association, 1970.

Institute of Chartered Accountants in England and Wales. *Accounting for Inflation.* London: Curven Press, 1973.

Internal Revenue Service. *Foreign Tax Credit for U.S. Citizens and Resident Aliens*, Publication 514. Washington, D.C.: U.S. Government Printing Office, 1975.

International Accounting Standards Committee. *Disclosure of Accounting Policies.* International Accounting Standard no. 1. London: IASC, 1974.

——. *Valuation and Presentation of Inventories in the Context of the Historical Cost System.* International Accounting Standard no. 2. London: IASC, 1975.

——. *Consolidated Financial Statements and the Equity Method of Accounting for Investments.* International Accounting Standard no. 3. London: IASC, 1976.

——. *Preface to Statements of International Accounting Standards.* London: IASC, 1974.

International Congress of Accountants. *New Horizons of Accounting.* Paris: International Congress of Accountants, 1967.

International Money Market of the Chicago Mercantile Exchange. *The Futures Market in Foreign Currencies*. Chicago: Chicago Mercantile Exchange, 1972.

Lathom-Sharp, I.N.S. "International Variations in Presentation and Certification of Accounts," *The Accountant* 165, no. 5040 (July 22, 1971): 124-26.

Lietaer, Bernard A. "Managing Risks in Foreign Exchange." *Harvard Business Review* 48, no. 2 (March-April 1970): 127-38.

Linowes, David F. "The Accounting Profession and Social Progress." *Journal of Accountancy* 136, no. 1 (July 1973): 32-40.

——. *The Corporate Conscience*. New York: Hawthorn Books, 1974.

Lorensen, Leonard. *Reporting Foreign Operations of U.S. Companies in U.S. Dollars*. Accounting Research Study no. 12. New York: American Institute of Certified Public Accountants, 1972.

Morgan Guaranty Trust Co. *Export and Import Procedures*. New York: Morgan Guaranty, 1968.

Mueller, Gerhard G. *International Accounting*. New York: Macmillan Company, 1967.

National Association of Accountants. *Management Accounting Problems in Foreign Operations*. N.A.A. Research Report 36. New York: NAA, 1960.

National Committee on Governmental Accounting. *Governmental Accounting, Auditing and Financial Reporting*. Chicago: Municipal Finance Officers Association, 1968.

National Foreign Trade Council. *Glossary of Foreign Trade Terms*. New York: National Foreign Trade Council, 1966.

Price Waterhouse & Co. *Information Guide: U.S. Corporations Doing Business Abroad*. New York: Price Waterhouse, 1975.

——. *Translation Procedures and Foreign Exchange*. New York: Price Waterhouse, 1975.

Price Waterhouse International. *Accounting Principles and Reporting Practices—A Survey in 38 Countries*. Toronto: Price Waterhouse, 1973.

Prindle, Andrean. "International Money Management—Systems and Techniques." *Euromoney*, October 1971, pp. 22-23.

Rosenfield, Paul. "General Price-Level Accounting and Foreign Financial Statements." *The Journal of Accountancy* 131, no. 2 (February 1971): 58-65.

Rueschhoff, Norlin G. "The Next Basic Financial Statement: The Statement of Shareholders' Equity." *The New York Certified Public Accountant* 41, no. 12 (January 1971): 887-90.

——. "U.S. Dollar Based Financial Reporting of Canadian Multinational Corporations." *The International Journal of Accounting* 8, no. 2 (Spring 1973): 103-09.

Salas, Cesar A. "Accounting, Education and Practice in Spanish Latin America." *The International Journal of Accounting* 3, no. 1 (Fall 1967): 67-85.

Scott, George M. *Accounting and Developing Nations.* Seattle: University of Washington, Graduate School of Business Administration, 1970.

———. *An Introduction to Financial Control and Reporting in Multinational Enterprises.* Austin: Bureau of Business Research, University of Texas, 1973.

Shulman, James. "When the Price is Wrong by Design." *Columbia Journal of World Business* 2, no. 3 (May-June 1967): 69-76.

Singhvi, Surendra S. *Corporate Financial Management in a Developing Economy.* Seattle: University of Washington, Graduate School of Business Administration, 1972.

Stabler, Charles N. "Controlling Cash." *Wall Street Journal*, May 19, 1972, pp. 1, 23.

U.S. Department of Commerce. *Foreign Direct Investment Regulations.* Washington, D.C.: U.S. Government Printing Office, June 1970.

Weirich, T. R., Clarence G. Avery, and Henry R. Anderson. "International Accounting, Varying Definitions." *The International Journal of Accounting* 7, no. 1 (Fall 1971): 79-87.

Williams, Bryan. "A Common European Currency." *Management in a World Perspective.* Los Angeles: School of Business, University of Southern California, 1975, pp. 30-39.

Wright, Richard W. "Trends in International Business Research." *Journal of International Business Studies* 1, no. 1 (Spring 1970): 109-23.

Zenoff, David B., and Jack Zwick. *International Financial Management.* Englewood Cliffs, N.J.: Prentice-Hall, 1969.

NORLIN G. RUESCHHOFF is associate professor of accountancy in the College of Business Administration at the University of Notre Dame, Notre Dame, Indiana.

At Notre Dame he has been instrumental in introducing the international accounting dimension into the undergraduate curriculum. He has served on the International Accounting Committee of the American Accounting Association, delivered several papers on international accounting education, acted as a consultant on international accounting principles and standards, and been employed as an international auditor and accountant.

Dr. Rueschhoff received his B.S.C. degree from Creighton University, his M.A. and Ph.D. degrees from the University of Nebraska, and C.P.A. certificate from the State of Nebraska. He was a student initiate in the Beta Gamma Sigma and Beta Alpha Psi honorary societies.

RELATED TITLES
Published by
Praeger Special Studies

FINANCIAL POLICIES FOR THE MULTINATIONAL
COMPANY: The Management of Foreign Exchange
Raj Aggarwal

*INTERNATIONAL FINANCIAL MARKETS: Development
of the Present System and Future Prospects
Francis A. Lees
Maximo Eng

INTERNATIONAL REGULATION OF MULTINATIONAL
CORPORATIONS
Don Wallace, Jr.

*THE MULTINATIONAL CORPORATION AND SOCIAL
CHANGE
edited by
David E. Apter
Louis Wolf Goodman

PRIVATE BANKING IN SWITZERLAND
P. J. Marczell

*Also available in paperback as a PSS Student Edition.